The Illative Imagination Through the Quill of Faith

Literary Paths to God in Newman and Hopkins

by

Dr. ant

The Illative Imagination Through the Quill of Faith: Literary Paths to God in Newman and Hopkins

Contents

Glossary

Introduction

In the vast expanse of human history and the intricate tapestry of theological discourse, two luminaries emerge with a profound impact on the understanding of faith through literature: John Henry Newman and Gerard Manley Hopkins. Their approaches, while distinct in essence, converge on the central premise of literature not merely as a medium for aesthetic pleasure but as a conduit of divine revelation. This exploration seeks to delve into the depths of their convictions, comparing and contrasting their perspectives on the nuanced relationship between literature and faith in God.

Faith, as illuminated in the scriptures, stands as the bedrock of believers' lives. "Now faith is the substance of things hoped for, the evidence of things not seen" (Heb. 11:1), presents faith as an assured confidence in the divine, a premise both Newman and Hopkins embraced with ardor. Yet, the journey of faith is not uniform; it meanders through the realms of intellect, emotion, and spirit, engaging individuals in a complex interplay of belief and understanding.

The concept of the illative sense, as articulated by Newman, posits a nuanced method of reasoning within the domain of faith, marrying intellect and intuition in the apprehension of divine truths. Literature, in this framework, emerges as a powerful illative instrument, capable of evoking a literary assent to faith. It is through the beauty of prose and poetry that the human soul encounters glimpses of the divine, prompting a response not solely of the mind but of the heart and spirit.

Gerard Manley Hopkins, with his unique literary craftsmanship, exemplifies the capability of literary forms to reflect the divine's intricate beauty. His innovative use of sprung rhythm and his profound theological insights woven through his poetry showcase literature's potential to evoke a deeper, more visceral understanding of God and His creation.

The exploration of Newman and Hopkins's perspectives reveals a compelling argument for literature as a vital pathway to God. It postulates that literature transcends mere entertainment or intellectual engagement; it serves as a vital illative sense, leading individuals to a deeper assent to faith, which in turn, fosters morality and evangelization. Such an argument places literature at the heart of theological discourse, suggesting that literary expressions of faith play a crucial role in the believer's journey towards understanding and embodying divine truths.

This discourse aims to resonate with a diverse audience, including college professors, Roman Catholics, literary scholars, and theologians, inviting them to reconsider the role of literature in the religious experience. It endeavors to provide a comprehensive examination of the literary and theological intersections in Newman and Hopkins's work, offering insights that bridge historical context and contemporary relevance.

As we traverse the literary landscapes crafted by these theological giants, we are invited to reflect upon our own journeys of faith. Literature becomes not just a mirror reflecting our spiritual quest but a lamp illuminating the path towards a deeper, more profound relationship with the divine. This examination seeks to inspire a renewed appreciation for the power of literature as a means of engaging with, understanding, and expressing our faith.

The intellectual and spiritual legacies of Newman and Hopkins serve as beacons, guiding us through the complexities of faith, reason, and literature. Their lives and works exemplify the profound impact that literature can have as a mediator of theological insights, illustrating the inseparable bond between literary expression and spiritual exploration.

By comparing and contrasting their approaches, this discourse endeavors to uncover the rich tapestry of connections between literature and faith, demonstrating how literary works can serve as vessels of divine truth and vehicles of moral and spiritual formation. The aim is not only to highlight the unique contributions of Newman and Hopkins but also to argue for the enduring relevance of literature in the pursuit of theological understanding and the expression of faith.

The contemplation of divine truths through literature invites us into a realm where faith and intellect converge, where the beauty of language and the profundity of belief intertwine. In exploring the literary paths to God laid out by Newman and Hopkins, we uncover broader insights into the nature of faith, the role of the intellect, and the power of literary expression in the spiritual life.

This journey through literature and theology is not merely an academic exercise; it is a pilgrimage of the mind and spirit. As we delve into the writings of Newman and Hopkins, we are reminded of the transformative power of literary engagement with faith, encouraging us to reflect on our own beliefs, experiences, and the ways in which literature informs and enriches our spiritual lives.

The juxtaposition of Newman and Hopkins's theological and literary insights offers a unique lens through which to view the intricate relationship between faith and literature. It challenges us to rethink the boundaries of theological discourse, recognizing the essential role of literary expression in exploring and communicating the mysteries of the divine.

In this exploration, literature emerges not only as a reflection of divine beauty and truth but also as an essential element of the believer's journey towards God. By engaging with literary works as pathways to divine encounter, we open ourselves to a deeper understanding of faith, a more profound appreciation of the divine, and a renewed commitment to expressing and living out our beliefs in the world.

In conclusion, the comparison and contrast of John Henry Newman and Gerard Manley Hopkins's approaches to faith in God through literature offer a compelling narrative of the transformative power of literary engagement with the divine. It is through literature that we can find a unique and powerful illative sense, leading us to an assent to faith that encompasses intellect, emotion, and spirit, and inspires a life of morality, evangelization, and service to God by employing our talents.

Chapter 1: The Meeting of Minds: An Overview of Newman and Hopkins

In the communion of sainthood, where thoughts traverse beyond the confines of time and space, the intellectual and spiritual camaraderie of John Henry Newman and Gerard Manley Hopkins flourishes. This chapter embarks on a journey through the intersecting orbits of these two colossal figures, navigating through their lives, their literary and theological landscapes, and the harmonies and dissonances between their understandings of faith and reason. It's through the prism of their shared faith that one can perceive the unique luminosity each brought into the realm of literature and theology, acting as vessels of divine truth in a world grappling with modernity's challenges.

Both Newman and Hopkins were men of their times, yet profoundly ahead of their epochs in understanding the interplay between the divine and the human, the eternal and the ephemeral. Newman, with his profound intellectual journey from Anglicanism to Roman Catholicism, exemplified the quest for truth through reason and faith, echoing the sentiment of St. Paul that we "prove all things; hold fast that which is good" (1 Thess. 5:21). Hopkins, on the other hand, captured the immanence of God in nature, finding the grandeur of the Creator in the pied beauty of the world. This was his lived theology, a resounding affirmation that "the earth is the Lord's, and the fulness thereof" (Psalm 24:1), manifest in each inscape and instress that his poetry so vividly depicted.

The confluence of their paths lies not just in their shared Catholic faith, but in their unwavering belief in literature as a means of divine revelation, a conviction that art and beauty are not mere adornments of life but essences of the Truth itself. This foundational belief underpins the discussions in the subsequent chapters, where their literary and theological methods, their philosophies of sin, redemption, and the use of creative gifts for evangelization are explored. As this overview unfolds, it becomes evident that Newman's illative sense and Hopkins's sprung rhythm are not merely academic concepts but lived experiences of faith. It is through the lens of their combined legacies that one can venture into a deeper understanding of how literature serves as a conduit to the divine, a theme that resonates through the ages and challenges the contemporary believer to ponder the sacred amidst the secular.

The Life and Times of John Henry Newman

The journey of faith is much like a river, winding and ever-evolving, its waters nourished by the rainfall of grace and the tributaries of divine revelation. In the vast ocean of Christian theology, John Henry Newman emerges as a river whose currents have carved out significant landscapes in the terrain of faith, reason, and literature. His life and times, a testament to the pursuit of truth and understanding, offer a rich field for exploration, especially when juxtaposed with the poetic genius of Gerard Manley Hopkins.

Newman's early life in London, marked by a rigorous academic upbringing and an early calling to the Anglican priesthood, laid the groundwork for his indelible impact on Christian theology. His intellect and spirit sought the divine in the intricate tapestry of religious belief and human reason, echoing the Psalms, "As the hart panteth after the water brooks, so panteth my soul after thee, O God" (Ps. 42:1). This thirst for a deeper understanding of the divine essence guided Newman through the varied phases of his spiritual journey.

The Oxford Movement, with which Newman became inextricably linked, marked a pivotal chapter in his story. This movement sought to return the Church of England to its apostolic roots, emphasizing a need for a revival of the rich traditions and doctrines that had been diluted over time. Newman's role as a leader in this movement showcased his profound belief in the importance of historical continuity and apostolic succession, aspects he believed were crucial for the true expression of Christian faith.

Yet, Newman's path was not one of linear progression but of complex evolution. His transition from Anglicanism to Roman Catholicism in 1845 was a profound turning point, underscored by his relentless pursuit of theological truth. This conversion was not merely a change in denominational affiliation but a transformative encounter with the mysteries of faith, akin to Paul's journey on the road to Damascus (Acts 9:3-6). Newman's embrace of Catholicism was met with controversy and criticism, yet it was through this crucible that his theological and literary contributions began to flourish.

At the heart of Newman's work was his concept of the illative sense, a principle that highlights the interplay between faith and reason. This principle posited that faith in God is arrived at not only through logical deduction but through a holistic engagement with the totality of human experience. Newman's elucidation of the illative sense in his seminal work, "An Essay in Aid of a Grammar of Assent," stands as one of his most enduring theological contributions, offering a nuanced understanding of how one comes to believe in the unseen.

Newman's ecclesiastical career, culminating in his elevation to Cardinal by Pope Leo XIII, was marked by his unwavering commitment to education and the development of the intellect. His founding of the Catholic University of Ireland and his authorship of "The Idea of a University" underscored his conviction that education was a vital conduit for both the exploration of faith and the cultivation of moral virtue.

In the realm of literature, Newman's mastery of the English language allowed him to articulate complex theological concepts with eloquence and clarity. His sermons, letters, and essays are suffused with a poetic sensitivity that lends them a timeless quality, while his novel "Loss and Gain" provides insight into the tumultuous journey of spiritual conversion.

Newman's later years were characterized by a period of prolific writing and reflection. His meditative work, "Apologia Pro Vita Sua," serves as a poignant autobiographical defense of his religious conversion and theological positions. Here, Newman laid bare his soul, inviting readers into the intimate struggles and triumphs of his faith journey.

The impact of Newman's life and works transcends his own era, speaking to the perennial challenges and aspirations of the human heart. His synthesis of faith and reason, tradition and innovation, serves as a beacon for those navigating the complexities of modern belief.

As Newman's journey unfolded, it became evident that his life was not just an exploration of theological truths but a testament to the power of divine grace acting through human frailty. "For when I am weak, then am I strong" (2 Cor. 12:10) encapsulates Newman's understanding that it is in our limitations that God's strength is most profoundly manifested.

In the dialogue between Newman and Hopkins, one finds a meeting of minds and spirits, each shaped by their unique encounters with the divine yet united in their belief in the transformative power of faith. Though their paths diverged in method and expression, at their core lay a shared conviction that literature and theology, when woven together, could illuminate the path to understanding and embracing the divine mystery.

Newman's legacy, deeply embedded in the tapestry of Christian thought and literary expression, continues to inspire and challenge. As a theologian, poet, and educator, he demonstrated that the journey of faith is not one of solitary contemplation but of engagement with the world in all its complexity and beauty.

It is in the confluence of Newman's and Hopkins' lives and works that one discovers a profound reflection on the nature of faith, the role of literature in spiritual formation, and the enduring quest for divine truth. This exploration not only enriches our understanding of their individual contributions but also offers insights into the ways in which literature can act as a channel for divine revelation and moral transformation.

Thus, the life and times of John Henry Newman stand as a testament to the enduring power of faith to shape human thought and history. In examining his journey, we are reminded of the profound mystery at the heart of Christian belief and the unending search for a deeper communion with the divine. The story of Newman's life and works remains a guiding light, illuminating the path for all who seek to navigate the complex interplay between faith, reason, and the illative sense in their pursuit of truth.

The Life and Times of Gerard Manley Hopkins

In the landscape of 19th-century literature and theology, Gerard Manley Hopkins stands as a figure whose contributions illuminate the intricate weave of faith and art. Born in 1844, into a world where the echoes of the Industrial Revolution clashed with a deep yearning for spiritual awakening, Hopkins' journey reflects a quest for divine beauty amidst the mechanization of life.

As a youth, Hopkins was deeply immersed in the Classics and the riches of English literature, displaying an early predilection for the aesthetic and spiritual. His path took a decisive turn upon his conversion to Roman Catholicism in 1866, a decision that marked not only a new spiritual beginning but also a vocational calling. This conversion was influenced profoundly by the works and person of John Henry Newman, whose embrace of Catholicism stirred in Hopkins both intrigue and inspiration.

The ordination of Hopkins as a Jesuit priest in 1877 was a further testament to his commitment to intertwining his intellectual pursuits with his spiritual life. Hopkins saw no distinction between the beauty found in the natural world and the divine, an outlook that fundamentally shaped his approach to poetry. It is in his verse that one finds the most compelling expressions of his theology, a theology profoundly incarnational, seeing in every landscape, every creature, a footprint of the Creator.

His innovation of sprung rhythm, a poetic technique that eschewed traditional metrics in favor of a more organic, speech-like pattern, stands as a testament to his belief in the uniqueness of God's creation, each syllable mirroring the unpredictability and splendor of the natural world.

Despite the brilliance of his work, Hopkins' poetry was not published or widely recognized during his lifetime. He labored in relative obscurity, a faithful servant whose duties often took him to challenging and isolating postings. His roles varied from teaching classics to young Jesuits in Wales to serving as a parish priest in inner-city Dublin. Yet, these experiences, far from being mere footnotes, were crucibles that forged his poetic voice, allowing him to explore the depths of human suffering and the redemptive beauty of faith.

Hopkins wrestled with the tension between his artistic temperament and the rigors of his religious vocation. This inner conflict often found expression in his poetry, where the palpable joy in creation coexists with a profound sense of desolation, a reflection of his personal trials and the spiritual aridity he sometimes experienced.

His masterpieces, such as "The Wreck of the Deutschland," "Pied Beauty," and "God's Grandeur," serve as eloquent defenses of God's presence in a world increasingly blinded by materialism and skepticism. Through his innovative use of language and form, Hopkins sought to awaken in his readers a sense of wonder and gratitude for the myriad ways in which the Creator speaks to His creation.

The legacy of Hopkins, like that of Newman, is found not only in the beauty of his words but in the lived testimony of his faith. In "As Kingfishers Catch Fire," Hopkins articulates a vision of Christ's presence in every aspect of life, insisting that each individual reflects the infinite creativity of God. Such a vision challenges the artificial division between sacred and secular, inviting a reintegration of faith with daily life.

While Hopkins did not live to see the impact of his work, his poetry eventually gained recognition, heralded for its daring style and profound spirituality. Today, Hopkins is celebrated as a pioneer, one who expanded the boundaries of English poetry and deepened the theological conversation through the medium of art.

Hopkins' life was an embodiment of the Psalmist's declaration, "O Lord, how manifold are thy works! in wisdom hast thou made them all: the earth is full of thy riches" (Psalm 104:24). In every petal, every wave, every human face, Hopkins discerned the handiwork of God, a reality he tirelessly sought to convey through his poetry.

In examining the lives of both Hopkins and Newman, it becomes evident that their approaches to faith, though distinct, share a common foundation: the conviction that the pursuit of truth and beauty leads one inevitably to the heart of divine mystery. For Hopkins, this pursuit was articulated through the vibrant tapestry of his verse, each line a testament to the immanence of God in the world.

The dialogue between faith and art that Hopkins engaged in is not merely an academic concern but a vital expression of the human search for meaning. In an era marked by uncertainty and change, Hopkins' work serves as a beacon, guiding those who wander in the shadows back to the light of God's presence.

As we reflect on the legacy of Gerard Manley Hopkins, we are reminded of the transformative power of beauty and the enduring call to see the world with the eyes of faith. His life and work stand as a testament to the possibility of encountering the divine in the everyday, urging us to "Give beauty back, beauty, beauty, beauty, back to God, beauty's self and beauty's giver" (Hopkins).

In conclusion, the life and poetry of Gerard Manley Hopkins offer a compelling narrative of the journey toward God, one that illuminates the path for all who seek to find in the beauty of the world a reflection of the divine Creator. The legacy he leaves is one of profound faith and artistic innovation, a beacon for those traversing the intersection of literature and theology in their quest for truth.

Intersecting Paths: Where Literature and Theology Meet

In traversing the storied landscapes of faith and literature, one ventures into a domain where the spiritual and the aesthetic converge, paving the way for a unique exploration of the Divine. This sacred journey, embarked upon by both John Henry Newman and Gerard Manley Hopkins, reveals the profound interconnection between literary expression and theological insight. Their lives, though rooted in different soils of time and experience, share a common thread - the weaving of words into a tapestry that captures the essence of divine encounter.

Newman, with his keen intellect and profound understanding of the human heart, saw literature not as mere ornamentation but as a channel through which the divine could be both sought and expressed. In his hands, words transcended their earthly origins, becoming a bridge to the ineffable. "But the natural man receiveth not the things of the Spirit of God: for they are foolishness unto him: neither can he know them, because they are spiritually discerned" (1 Cor. 2:14). For Newman, literature served as a means to spiritually discern and articulate the truths of faith, making the intangible tangibly felt through the beauty of language.

Similarly, Hopkins, a poet of exquisite sensitivity and fervor, found in the natural world a canvas upon which the light of God was brilliantly reflected. His poetry, marked by the innovative use of sprung rhythm, becomes an act of worship, a testament to the presence of the Creator in the minutiae of creation. Psalm 19:1 declares, "The heavens declare the glory of God; and the firmament sheweth his handywork." Hopkins echoed this sentiment, seeing in the dappled things of the earth a reflection of divine beauty and grace. Through his verse, theology and nature entwine, each illuminating the other.

The confluence of literature and theology in the works of Newman and Hopkins underscores a shared belief: that art and faith are not mere acquaintances but intimate friends, each enriching the other. Their literary endeavors were not just acts of creative expression but also profound acts of faith, an offering of their intellect and imagination to God. In their writings, we witness a dialogue between the soul and its Creator, mediated through the written word. This dialogue, rich in symbolism and imagery, invites readers into a deeper contemplation of the divine mystery.

Yet, while both men harnessed the power of literature to explore theological themes, their paths were uniquely their own. Newman, navigating the tumults of doubt and certainty, utilized literature as a means to argue and persuade, to address the intellect as well as the heart. His approach reflects a journey from skepticism to faith, a journey that finds its resolution in the embrace of the Catholic Church. Through this journey, literature becomes a lantern, illuminating the path to truth and understanding.

Contrastingly, Hopkins' poetic journey is one of awe and wonder, a celebration of God's creation as revealed through the natural world. His poetry, vibrant and alive with the joy of discovery, serves as a reminder that divine mystery enfolds us at every moment, if only we have eyes to see and ears to hear. Hopkins' works invite us to gaze upon the world with the fresh vision of a heart in love with God, to see in every landscape and creature a reflection of divine beauty.

The legacy of Newman and Hopkins, their intersection of faith and literature, challenges us to consider the role of art in our own spiritual journey. As we engage with their writings, we are invited to reflect on how beauty, imagination, and creativity can draw us closer to the Divine. Their works serve as beacons, guiding us to a deeper understanding of God's presence in our lives and in the world around us.

In this confluence of literature and theology, we find a rich soil for contemplation and dialogue. The intersection of Newman and Hopkins' paths offers us a lens through which to view the transformative power of faith and the arts. It reminds us that literature can be an avenue of discovery, a way to encounter God not just in the abstract but in the concrete realities of our human experience.

As we delve deeper into their writings, we encounter a multifaceted conversation about the nature of God, the beauty of creation, and the journey of faith. This conversation transcends the boundaries of time and place, inviting us into a timeless communion with the Divine. It is a conversation that beckons us to recognize the sacred in the ordinary, to find in the rhythm of words and the imagery of poetry a reflection of the infinite.

The enduring relevance of Newman and Hopkins' literary and theological explorations lies in their ability to speak to the human condition, to address the yearnings of the heart and the questions of the mind. In a world often marked by disconnection and disarray, their works offer a sanctuary, a place of respite and reflection. They remind us that in the act of creating and engaging with literature, we participate in the ongoing dialogue between Creator and creation.

Ultimately, the intersection of literature and theology as embodied by Newman and Hopkins invites us to reexamine our own approach to faith and creativity. It challenges us to consider how we, too, can use our talents and insights to explore the divine, to bring forth beauty that beckons others to look beyond the surface of things. In their confluence of paths, we find not just a meeting of minds but a convergence of souls, united in their quest for the transcendent.

As stewards of this rich heritage, we are called to continue the exploration, to weave our own narratives of faith and art. In doing so, we honor the legacy of Newman and Hopkins, joining them in the sacred task of illuminating the Divine through the beauty of the written word. For in the melding of literature and theology, we find a pathway to understanding, a bridge to the ineffable, a testament to the enduring power of faith and the arts to shape, inform, and transform our world.

Therefore, let us take up the pen and the prayer with equal fervor, that through our words and our works, we might reflect the light of the Divine, illuminating the path for those who seek to journey deeper into the mystery of faith. "Thy word is a lamp unto my feet, and a light unto my path" (Psalm 119:105). In this sacred endeavor, literature and theology meet, forging a path of beauty and truth that leads us, ever closer, to the heart of God.

Chapter 2: The Illative Sense Defined

In delving further into the theological discourse, an imperative concept arises from the nexus of divinity and reason, termed as the illative sense. This term, imbued with the profundity of human cognition and divine inference, constructs a bridge between the realms of faith and rational discourse. The Scripture elucidates this intertwining of belief and intellect in Proverbs, stating, "The heart of the prudent getteth knowledge; and the ear of the wise seeketh knowledge" (Prov. 18:15). Thus, the illative sense surfaces not merely as an intellectual inclination but as a profound disposition of heart and spirit towards discerning truth.

At its core, the illative sense encompasses a faculty of judgment, a capability to sift through a myriad of observations, experiences, and testimonies to arrive at a conclusive standpoint, especially in contexts bereft of empirical proofs. It resembles the act of navigation through a fog enshrouded landscape, where one must rely on the subtle signs and innate senses to discern the path forward. In the domain of faith, this navigational tool allows believers to traverse the nebulous junction between seen and unseen, tangibly expressing faith in God amidst the ineffable mystery of the divine. "For we walk by faith, not by sight" (2 Cor. 5:7) captures this journey's essence, where the illative sense is the compass guiding the soul's passage.

Central to this discourse is the proposition that literature, with its profound capacity to evoke introspection, empathy, and understanding, serves as the main vehicle for the illative sense. This literary assent to faith is not an abandonment of reason but rather its highest calling, where one engages with texts and narratives that transcend the mere concatenation of words, fostering a moral and spiritual awakening. Literature, in this light, becomes a sanctified medium, echoing the biblical parable of the sower, where seeds of faith are sown in the fertile soil of the human heart (Matt. 13:3-9).

Thus, the illative sense defined herein posits literature as a critical instrument of evangelization, a means through which one's talents are channeled towards the service of God and humanity. It embodies a literary assent to faith, a conviction that navigates through the subtleties and nuances of human experiences and expressions, guiding one towards a deeper moral comprehension and spiritual enlightenment. This sense, therefore, acts as a beacon, illuminating the path towards divine truth and moral rectitude.

In conclusion, as we further dissect and explore the illative sense, it is imperative to highlight its role as a conduit towards faith, facilitated by the eloquent power of literature. This synthesis of faith and reason, guided by the illative sense, fosters a unique appreciation for the divine, transcending the conventional boundaries of theological discourse. It beckons believers towards a higher calling, where literary engagement becomes an act of faith and an expression of the soul's deepest yearnings for the divine. "Thy word is a lamp unto my feet, and a light unto my path" (Ps. 119:105), epitomizes this spiritual journey, where the illative sense enriches our moral and spiritual landscapes, guiding us towards eternal truths.

Understanding Newman's Concept

The illative sense, as introduced by John Henry Newman, encompasses a method of reasoning which is profoundly personal and intricately bound to the subjective experience of the individual. This concept, deeply philosophical yet accessible, invites the exploration of truth through the nuanced lens of personal judgment and discernment. At the heart of Newman's philosophy lies the assertion that truth, especially religious truth, cannot be fully encapsulated by empirical evidence or logical deductions alone.

Consider the words of the Apostle Paul, "For we walk by faith, not by sight" (2 Cor. 5:7). This scripture poignantly echoes Newman's understanding of the illative sense; it is faith that guides our understanding and not merely what is tangible. Newman's emphasis on the personal dimension of discernment and belief espouses a view of faith that is both dynamically engaged with the intellect and deeply rooted in the spiritual experience of the believer.

The illative sense, therefore, operates within the realms of both intellect and intuition, offering a pathway through which one may navigate the complexities of theological and moral truth. It's a sense that combines the objective with the subjective, allowing for a conviction of faith that is both informed and deeply personal. Newman illustrates this through his notion of certitude, suggesting that true certainty in faith arises from a holistic engagement with truth, involving both the mind and the heart.

In the contemporary context of faith and reason, Newman's concept provides a refreshing alternative to the often polarized views on the matter. He posits that faith is not against reason but rather complements it, providing a foundation upon which reason can rest and flourish. This idea is critically important in an era that frequently witnesses an imbalance, favoring either empirical evidence or blind faith.

Newman's illative sense, though personal, is not entirely subjective or relativistic. It is grounded in the objective reality of God's existence and the truth of the Christian faith. This balance offers a powerful counterpoint to modern tendencies toward skepticism and relativism, suggesting that faith in God involves an integrative process that encompasses both the mind and the heart.

The relevance of the illative sense in understanding religious belief cannot be overstated. It offers a robust framework for navigating the complexities of faith in a rational and deeply personal manner. Newman's concept challenges believers to engage their intellect in their spiritual journey, embracing a thoughtful and discerning approach to their belief system.

Moreover, the illative sense has significant implications for evangelization and apologetics. It provides a method for articulating and defending the faith that is both intellectually credible and personally meaningful. In a world where religious beliefs are often scrutinized and challenged, Newman's approach offers a viable pathway for presenting Christianity in a manner that is reasoned and relatable.

The philosophical underpinings of the illative sense also have profound implications for morality. Newman suggests that moral judgments, like religious beliefs, involve a complex process of discernment that cannot be reduced to simple formulas or rules. This perspective encourages a moral framework that is flexible and responsive to the nuances of personal experience and societal context.

For scholars and theologians, Newman's concept opens up new avenues for exploring the interaction between faith and reason, as well as the role of personal judgment in religious belief. It challenges traditional apologetics to move beyond formulaic arguments to a more nuanced engagement with the complexities of faith.

The illative sense also speaks to the heart of literature and the arts as pathways to understanding God. It suggests that creativity and imagination are not merely decorative aspects of human experience but are central to how we perceive and engage with truth. This aligns perfectly with those who view literature and the arts as essential dimensions of revealing divine truth.

In conclusion, Newman's concept of the illative sense offers a rich and multifaceted approach to faith, reason, and morality. It champions a view of Christianity that is intellectually rigorous, personally meaningful, and deeply rooted in the human experience. In a world that often seems fragmented by differing views on faith and reason, Newman's vision provides a compelling framework for unity and understanding.

The exploration of Newman's illative sense thus provides not only a pathway to comprehend the complex interplay between faith and reason but also a lens through which we can view the world, informed by a faith that seeks understanding, as Augustine once described it. It's a journey that invites both the heart and mind to venture together in search of the divine presence that permeates all of existence.

As we delve further into the implications of the illative sense for modern believers, we find a concept that remains as relevant and vital today as it was in Newman's time. It offers a beacon of hope and a call to deeper engagement with our faith, challenging us to a fuller, more integrated understanding of our belief in God. The illative sense, thus understood, becomes not only a personal journey of faith but a testament to the enduring power of belief to transcend the boundaries of reason and touch the heart of human existence.

Therefore, in embracing Newman's concept, we find ourselves drawn into a more profound and comprehensive approach to spirituality. It's an approach that acknowledges the complexities of human cognition and the depth of the spiritual journey, inviting us to a richer, more nuanced understanding of our relationship with the divine. This exploration into the illative sense is more than an academic exercise; it is an invitation to a deeper, more authentic engagement with faith itself.

Literary Assent and Faith

In the contemplation of faith and reason, we arrive at a juncture where literature serves not merely as an artistic endeavor but as the vessel through which the Divine whispers to the human soul. The essence of literary assent lies in the profound recognition that the truths of faith often find their most compelling expression through the narrative and poetic forms. This is where the illative sense, as outlined in previous discussions, converges with the spiritual journey, offering a path that leads one to God through the beauty and depth of literary craft.

The scriptures themselves bear witness to the power of word and narrative, for "In the beginning was the Word, and the Word was with God, and the Word was God" (John 1:1). Herein lies the foundational belief that God Himself chose the literary form as the prime medium of revelation to humanity. This precedence underscores the intrinsic value of literature in the discourse of faith, illuminating the path for believers to engage with the Divine through the written word.

Literary works possess the unique capability to mirror the complexities of human existence, thereby fostering a profound empathy and moral reflection that resonate with the reader's own spiritual journey. In the nuanced interplay of character, conflict, and resolution, literature invites its audience into a deeper contemplation of virtue, vice, and the overarching quest for meaning and redemption. Thus, the act of reading becomes an act of faith—a willing assent to the truths embedded within the narrative, truths that echo the eternal.

This assent is not passive but involves an active engagement of the intellect and the heart, allowing the reader to discern and embrace deeper theological and moral insights. The narrative or poetic structure serves as a vessel, channeling the reader's contemplation towards the ineffable, towards an encounter with the Divine that transcends the mere accumulation of doctrinal knowledge. Such is the power of literary expression that it can unveil the grandeur of God in the subtleties of human experience.

Moreover, the creation of literature itself emerges as an expression of faith. The writer, as a co-creator with the Divine, engages in an act of faith with each stroke of the pen, each crafting of metaphor and narrative. Through the imaginative exploration of truth, beauty, and goodness, literature offers a distinctive mode of expressing and experiencing God's presence in the world.

In this context, the illative sense, as the faculty of reasoning that engages with the non-formal inferences of the heart and the imagination, finds in literature a fertile ground for its operation. It is in the aesthetic and moral dimensions of literature that the heart discerns the whispers of the Spirit, guiding the intellect towards a holistic understanding of faith that encompasses both reason and the ineffable movements of the soul.

The literary assent to faith, then, is not an abandonment of reason but its fulfillment. It embodies a recognition that the truths of faith, while transcending empirical verification, are no less real for their mystery. They demand a form of knowing and assenting that engages the whole person—mind, heart, and imagination.

This holistic engagement fosters a moral and spiritual transformation in the reader, who, through the act of reading, participates in the drama of salvation history. Literature becomes a threshold over which the reader steps into a deeper communion with the Divine, encountering through the lives of characters and the beauty of the created world, a call to live out the virtues of faith, hope, and love.

Thus, literary assent to faith nurtures not only a personal transformation but has implications for evangelization and moral action within the community. In reflecting upon and sharing the insights gained through literature, believers can inspire one another towards greater love and service to God and neighbor, fulfilling the call to be the light of the world and the salt of the earth (Matt. 5:13-14).

The integration of literature and faith, therefore, serves as a conduit for both personal and communal renewal. It offers a pathway for encountering God through the beauty and complexity of human experience, articulated through the power of narrative and poetry. This interweaving of faith and literature enriches the spiritual journey, opening hearts to the Divine mystery that surpasses all understanding yet seeks to be known in the depths of the human soul.

In conclusion, the literary assent to faith is a testament to the boundless ways in which God reveals Himself to humanity. It affirms the truth that the search for God and the expression of faith are not confined to the walls of churches or the pages of theological treatises but are woven into the very fabric of human culture and creativity. Literature, with its capacity to convey the transcendent within the immanent, stands as a vital means by which the illative sense draws the soul towards the ultimate Truth that is God.

Therefore, it behooves us to approach literature with an openness to the Divine, recognizing in the stories we read and write the potential for a deeper encounter with the One who is both Author and Finisher of our faith (Heb. 12:2). In this way, literary assent becomes a channel of grace, illuminating the path to God through the power of the written word, and beckoning us to live our lives as a reflection of that transcendent truth, beauty, and goodness we encounter therein.

Chapter 3: Literature as a Pathway to God

In the tapestry of human endeavor, literature stands as one of the most profound expressions of the soul's journey towards the divine. It serves not only as a mirror reflecting the complexities of human experience but also as a bridge connecting the human spirit with the transcendental realities of faith. The sacred scriptures themselves testify to the power of the written word as a conduit of divine truth: "For the word of God is quick, and powerful, and sharper than any twoedged sword" (Heb. 4:12). In the context of this truth, one can apprehend the significance of literature as a pathway to God, a theme deeply embedded in the works and thoughts of both John Henry Newman and Gerard Manley Hopkins.

Newman, with his profound understanding of the human heart and its inclinations, employed literature to illustrate faith, making the invisible visible through the beauty and depth of language. He believed that literature could serve as a medium to express the complexities and nuances of faith in a manner that resonates with the human experience. For him, the narrative and poetic forms become vessels of divine truth, capable of moving the soul toward a deeper recognition and appreciation of the divine presence in the world. The illuminative power of literature, in Newman's perspective, lies in its ability to captivate the imagination and direct the heart towards the contemplation of higher truths.

On the other hand, Hopkins, a poet par excellence, utilized the aesthetic force of words to reveal the presence of God in the natural world. His poetic innovations, such as the use of sprung rhythm, served to evoke the dynamic and vivacious quality of God's creation, inviting the reader to perceive the divine footprint in all things. "The world is charged with the grandeur of God," declares Hopkins (Pied Beauty), a revelation captured not through doctrinal exposition but through the lyrical exuberance of his poetry. Through Hopkins' eyes, literature becomes not just a pathway but an actual encounter with God, manifested in the minute details of nature and the profound experiences of human life.

The contemplation of literature as a pathway to God necessitates a recognition of its power to transform the intellect and will. By engaging with texts that bear the imprint of divine truth, one embarks on a journey that transcends mere intellectual assent, venturing into the heart's sanctum where faith and reason converge. Literature, in its highest form, acts as a catalyst that awakens the desire for God, planting seeds of eternity in the human heart. As such, it holds the potential not only to inform but to form, shaping the soul's disposition towards the divine.

In the final analysis, the exploration of literature as a pathway to God reveals its intrinsic value not merely as an academic discipline but as a profound spiritual exercise. Through the literary corpus of Newman and Hopkins, we discern a vibrant testament to the possibility of encountering God in the realm of words and imagination. In this light, literature serves as a beacon, guiding the soul through the vicissitudes of life towards the ultimate horizon of faith, where the Word, who is "the light of men" (John 1:4), illuminates the path to salvation and sanctity. Thus, in the embrace of literature, one finds not only aesthetic or intellectual satisfaction but a deepened capacity for divine communion, embodying the profoundest aspiration of the human heart towards the eternal.

Newman's Use of Literature to Illustrate Faith

In the realm of faith and reason, literature emerges not merely as an art form but as a profound interpreter of the divine mystery. Through the lens of John Henry Newman, literature transcends its aesthetic bounds to become a vital conduit to the divine, illustrating faith in a manner no simple didactic exposition could achieve. It is this recognition of literature's unique power that forms the crux of Newman's approach to illustrating faith.

For Newman, literature served as a mirror to the human soul, reflecting its complexities, its quest for truth, and its grappling with the mysteries of existence and the divine. He discerned in literature a distinct capacity to articulate the ineffable, to bring forth into the light of comprehension truths which otherwise remained cloaked in obscurity. It was through the narrative, the poetic, and the symbolic that Newman believed one could encounter the divine in a space beyond the limitations of empirical proof or dogmatic assertion.

At the heart of Newman's utilization of literature was his profound belief in the power of storytelling. He understood that stories, parables, and allegories had the unique capacity to communicate truths about God and faith that were otherwise impenetrable. This belief is deeply rooted in the biblical tradition, as evidenced by Christ's use of parables to elucidate the mysteries of the Kingdom of Heaven. Newman, in his alignment with this biblical precedent, recognized that "the kingdom of God is like unto a treasure hid in a field" (Matt. 13:44), suggesting that truths about faith often require excavation through narrative and symbol.

Moreover, Newman's appreciation for literature was intricately linked to his broader theological insights. He held that the journey towards understanding and embracing faith was inherently personal and subjective, a journey that literature could both mirror and facilitate. In this way, literature becomes a pathway to God, offering a journey through which one encounters the divine mystery not as an abstract concept but as a lived, felt experience. For Newman, literature was not just illustrative of faith; it was integral to the very process of faith's realization.

Newman's use of literature also demonstrated his commitment to the idea that truth transcends empirical evidence and rational proof. In an age increasingly dominated by scientific positivism, Newman stood as a countercurrent, advocating for the validity of truth known through conscience, experience, and, significantly, through literary engagement. He posited that literature could awaken the conscience and stimulate the moral imagination, thereby opening the heart and mind to the truths of faith. In this view, literature becomes a gateway to an encounter with the divine, a means through which one can come to a deeper understanding and acceptance of God's presence in the world.

But Newman's vision for literature was not merely about personal edification or the nurturing of individual faith. He perceived in literature a potent means of evangelization, a way to engage the culture at large with the truths of the Christian faith. Through compelling narratives, characters, and images, literature could speak to the heart in a language that rationale discourse could not, potentially drawing souls closer to God. This evangelistic potential of literature underscores Newman's drive to integrate literary engagement with the broader mission of the Church.

Newman's discernment of the connections between literature and faith led him to engage deeply with a broad range of literary works, both sacred and secular. He held that even secular literature, when approached with discernment, could illumine aspects of the divine and the moral landscape of the human condition. This openness to finding glimpses of truth in unexpected places reflects Newman's conviction that God's grace operates throughout all creation, and that insights into faith can emerge in the myriad expressions of human creativity.

Furthermore, Newman's embrace of literature as a pathway to God was marked by an earnest engagement with ancient classical literature as well as the works of his contemporaries. He recognized in the classics a deep wellspring of wisdom on human nature, virtue, and the divine, while contemporary works provided a mirror to the spiritual and moral questions of his own time. This dual engagement allowed Newman to bridge the timeless with the timely, providing perspectives on faith that were at once rooted in tradition and responsive to contemporary challenges.

In Newman's view, literature also served an apologetic function, defending the truths of the Christian faith against skepticism and disbelief. By presenting the beauty, complexity, and depth of faith through literary forms, he sought to counter the prevailing narratives of secularism and materialism. It is in the beauty of a poem, the depth of a novel's characters, or the moral struggles depicted in a play that Newman found compelling evidence of the reality of God's presence and action in the world.

This apologetic aspect of Newman's engagement with literature was not about simplistic propaganda or reductionist portrayals of faith. Rather, it involved presenting the rich tapestry of human experience in relation to the divine, including doubts, struggles, and complexities. For Newman, the authenticity of these portrayals was crucial in illustrating the truth of faith in a way that resonated with the realities of human life.

Moreover, Newman's literary approach to faith did not shy away from the complexities and paradoxes inherent in human existence and the divine mystery. He understood that literature could hold tension, ambiguity, and mystery in a way that doctrinal formulations could not. This capacity of literature to embrace and explore complexities made it an ideal medium through which to approach the mysterious nature of God and the intricacies of faith.

In essence, Newman's engagement with literature was a testament to his conviction that faith is not a matter of abstract dogma but a lived, experiential reality. He saw in literature a unique vehicle for expressing, exploring, and encountering this reality, a means of drawing both the individual and the community closer to the infinite mystery of God. Through his writings and his approach to literature, Newman invites us on a journey of faith, one that acknowledges the power of story, symbol, and narrative to illuminate the path to the divine.

Newman's integration of literature into his understanding of faith was a pioneering effort to bridge the perceived chasm between the sacred and the secular, between reason and imagination. In doing so, he offered a vision of faith that is richly textured, deeply human, and profoundly engaging, a vision that continues to inspire and challenge believers and seekers alike. Through his discerning and thoughtful engagement with literature, Newman not only illustrated faith but also enriched the broader conversation about what it means to believe, to doubt, and ultimately, to know God.

The legacy of Newman's use of literature to illustrate faith thus stands as a beacon to all who are navigating the complex interplay of faith, culture, and creativity. It serves as a reminder that in the realm of the spirit, the power of the word, in all its literary forms, remains an enduring pathway to the heart of the divine mystery. This is Newman's enduring gift to the faithful and the inquiring mind alike: the recognition that literature, in its profound capacity to reflect and shape the human soul, holds within it the luminous threads of divine revelation.

Hopkins' Literary Contributions to Theology

The intersection of literature and theology is a fertile ground for exploring the intricacies of faith, and Gerard Manley Hopkins's oeuvre stands as a monumental testament to this synergy. Through his pioneering use of language and form, Hopkins not only revolutionized English poetry but also offered a unique lens through which the divine can be contemplated. His poetry, brimming with a profound sense of God's presence in the natural world, invites readers into a space of theological reflection that transcends conventional religious discourse.

Hopkins's engagement with theology through literature was not merely incidental but intentional and deeply integrated into his poetic vision. His works are often seen as a vibrant tapestry of aesthetic beauty and theological depth, weaving together insights into God's creation, human experience, and the quest for transcendence. This synthesis is perhaps most evident in his concept of "inscape," the distinctive design that individual beings and objects possess, which reveals the divine intentionality behind creation.

In contemplating Hopkins's literary contributions to theology, it is essential to recognize the influence of his Jesuit formation. The Ignatian spirituality that informed his worldview placed a strong emphasis on finding God in all things. For Hopkins, the act of poetic creation became a means of discerning and celebrating the divine presence in the everyday, turning the mundane into a source of spiritual revelation.

Hopkins's use of sprung rhythm, a metric innovation that accentuates the natural cadences of speech, serves as a theological tool, mirroring the dynamic and unpredictable nature of God's grace. This rhythmic departure from conventional verse forms allows for a richer expression of awe and wonder at the divine, creating an immersive experience that invites readers to enter more deeply into the mystery of faith.

His poem "Pied Beauty" exemplifies how Hopkins's literary artistry contributes to theology. The poem's praise for the "dappled things" of the world becomes a hymn to the creator's boundless imagination and benevolence. Through his vivid imagery and playful language, Hopkins opens up a space for contemplating the diversity of God's creation as a reflection of divine glory. "For all things counter, original, spare, strange; / Whatever is fickle, freckled (who knows how?) / With swift, slow; sweet, sour; adazzle, dim; / He fathers-forth whose beauty is past change: / Praise him" ("Pied Beauty").

The theme of God's immanence and transcendence runs deep in Hopkins's poetry, providing a nuanced theological reflection on the nature of divine reality. His vivid descriptions of natural phenomena are not merely aesthetic observations but are imbued with a sense of sacramental vision, where the material world becomes a transparent vehicle of God's grace.

In "God's Grandeur," Hopkins marvels at the resilience of God's presence in the world despite humanity's neglect and abuse of creation. The poem recognizes the enduring nature of divine grace, asserting that the Holy Ghost over the bent world broods with warm breast and with ah! bright wings. This portrays a deeply incarnational understanding of God's relationship with the world, emphasizing a continuity between the material and the spiritual.

Hopkins's engagement with the problem of evil and suffering also highlights his theological contributions. In poems such as "Carrion Comfort," he explores the depths of despair and the feeling of abandonment by God, yet he also witnesses to the redemptive potential of suffering. This wrestling with darkness and light reflects a profound engagement with the Paschal mystery, the death and resurrection of Jesus Christ, as a central tenet of Christian faith.

Furthermore, Hopkins's attention to the individual experience, as seen in his portraits of people and landscapes, underscores a theology of personalism. His poetry affirms the unique value and dignity of each being as a reflection of the Creator, challenging the impersonal and mechanistic views of the world that were emerging in his time.

The environmental consciousness evident in Hopkins's work also contributes to contemporary theological discussions on creation care. His sense of wonder at the natural world and his grief over its degradation resonate with current calls for ecological stewardship as a moral and spiritual responsibility.

Hopkins's poetry, steeped in theological insight, challenges the modern reader to see the world anew through the lens of faith. It is a call to marvel at the grandeur of God's creation, to wrestle with the mysteries of suffering and redemption, and to recognize the sacred in the ordinary. In doing so, Hopkins's literary contributions to theology extend an invitation to explore the depth and breadth of the divine mystery, urging a reawakening to the presence of God in all aspects of life.

In conclusion, Gerard Manley Hopkins's literary contributions to theology are as groundbreaking as they are profound. By weaving together the threads of aesthetic beauty, personal experience, and theological reflection, Hopkins opens up new vistas for understanding the relationship between God and the world. His poetry serves as a beacon for those navigating the complex terrain of faith, offering both solace and challenge. Hopkins reminds us that literature can be a pathway to God, illuminating the divine presence in the tapestry of creation and inviting us into a deeper engagement with the mysteries of faith.

Chapter 4: The Intellect and Will in Newman's Theology

In the heart of Newman's theological exegesis, the interplay between intellect and will serves as an essential foundation upon which faith and reason build a symbiotic relationship. This union, as articulated, champions the principle that belief in God is neither solely an act of intellectual assent nor purely a matter of willful decision, but rather, a harmonious cooperation of both faculties. As it is written, "Thou shalt love the Lord thy God with all thy heart, and with all thy soul, and with all thy mind" (Matt. 22:37), so does Newman's theology emphasize that the mind and the heart must work in concert to apprehend the divine truth fully.

The role of reason within faith, according to Newman, is not to prove the existence of God beyond the shadow of a doubt but to provide a rational foundation for belief that complements and extends beyond the empirical evidence. As the psalmist implores, "Come and see the works of God" (Psalm 66:5), Newman invites the faithful to perceive the presence of the divine through the lens of reason enlightened by faith. It is this invitation to "see" that encapsulates Newman's proposition: faith and reason are not adversaries but allies in the soul's journey towards understanding and embracing the transcendent.

Moreover, Newman underscores the importance of moral agency and the divine call to serve, elucidating how the will, shaped by the moral intellect, propels individuals toward acts of love and service in the imitation of Christ. This perspective foregrounds the notion that true belief manifests in action, reflecting the biblical injunction, "Even so faith, if it hath not works, is dead, being alone" (James 2:17). Consequently, Newman's theological vision casts the intellect and will not as mere facets of human nature but as instruments of divine grace, guiding the believer to respond to God's call with both mind and heart, thereby integrating faith into every aspect of life.? Through this integration, Newman articulates a comprehensive vision of Christian living that marries the cognitive and volitional aspects of faith, highlighting his profound understanding of the complex dynamics that underpin the human quest for God.

The Role of Reason in Faith

In exploring the intricate tapestry that interweaves the intellect and will within Newman's theological framework, one cannot overlook the paramount role that reason plays in the development and expression of faith. This discourse endeavors to unravel the complexities surrounding reason's contribution to faith, drawing upon scriptural insights, theological profundity, and philosophical acumen. In doing so, it will become apparent how reason is not merely an auxiliary to faith but rather an indispensable component that enriches and deepens one's relationship with the Divine.

At the outset, it is imperative to comprehend that reason and faith are not adversaries vying for the supremacy of the human soul, but are rather harmonious allies in the quest for truth. "Come now, and let us reason together, saith the Lord" (Isa. 1:18), serves as a testament to the intrinsic value that the scripture places on reason as a medium through which humanity can engage with the divine will. This invitation to reason with God underscores the compatibility of faith and intellect, suggesting that divine truths are accessible to human comprehension and rational investigation.

However, in appreciating the role of reason in faith, one must acknowledge its limitations. Reason, while powerful, cannot fathom the mysteries of faith in their entirety. Faith transcends human understanding, as it is written, "For my thoughts are not your thoughts, neither are your ways my ways, saith the Lord" (Isa. 55:8). This does not diminish the value of reason but rather situates it within its proper context: as a guide, a light illuminating the path to greater understanding, not the final destination.

One of the principal functions of reason within the realm of faith is discernment. Reason aids believers in distinguishing truth from falsehood, enabling them to navigate the complexities of modernity with a grounded sense of morality and spirituality. This discernment is not born out of skepticism but rather from a profound desire to align one's beliefs and actions with the truth revealed through Scripture and Tradition.

In the dynamic interplay between intellect and will, reason serves as a catalyst for a more profound and mature faith. It prompts one to ask questions, to seek understanding, and to delve deeper into the mysteries of the divine. This intellectual pursuit does not lead to a fragmented faith but to an integrated spirituality that embraces both the known and the unknown, recognizing that "Now we see through a glass, darkly; but then face to face" (1 Cor. 13:12).

Furthermore, reason enriches faith by opening a dialogue with culture, science, and other realms of human knowledge. This engagement is not a concession but a confident assertion of faith's ability to absorb truth from all sources, as "All truth is God's truth." Reason, therefore, becomes the bridge that connects faith with broader human experience, enhancing its relevance and applicability in the contemporary world.

It is also through reason that faith communicates its profound truths to others. Persuasion, grounded in logical argument and evidence, remains a crucial tool in evangelization. Through reasoned discourse, faith articulates its claims in a manner that is comprehensible and compelling to others, thereby fulfilling the mandate to "be ready always to give an answer to every man that asketh you a reason of the hope that is in you with meekness and fear" (1 Pet. 3:15).

Moreover, reason aids in the interpretation of Scripture, helping believers discern the spiritual truths concealed within the sacred texts. Through exegesis, guided by reason and enlightened by the Holy Spirit, the Word of God becomes a living dialogue that speaks into the lives of believers across ages and cultures.

In grappling with the problem of evil and suffering, reason provides a framework for understanding these realities within the larger narrative of salvation history. Though it cannot provide all the answers, reason helps to maintain faith's integrity in the face of doubt and despair, offering perspectives that affirm God's sovereignty and ultimate goodness.

Finally, reason enhances the worship experience. Understanding the theological and historical significance of liturgical practices deepens one's appreciation and engagement with the worship act, transforming it from a mere ritual into a meaningful encounter with the living God.

In conclusion, reason's role within the landscape of faith is multifaceted and profound. It acts as a navigator, assisting believers in their spiritual journey towards an ever-deepening understanding of divine truths. By embracing reason, the believer engages more fully with their faith, experiencing its richness and depth in a manner that is intellectually satisfying and spiritually fulfilling. Thus, reason and faith, far from being at odds, are inextricably linked, each elevating and enriching the other in the pursuit of truth and the expression of divine love.

In the grand narrative of salvation, reason and faith coalesce into a symphony of understanding, where the mysteries of God are engaged with the fullness of the human spirit. This harmonious interplay enables a faith that is both thoughtfully considered and deeply felt, offering a beacon of light in a world that often seems shrouded in darkness and doubt.

Therefore, in the theology espoused by Newman, the intellect and will, guided by reason and nourished by faith, converge towards a singular end: the profound and transformative encounter with the Divine. It is in this sacred meeting place that the human heart finds its truest expression and its deepest fulfillment.

Moral Agency and the Call to Serve

In delving into the heart of moral agency according to the theological insights of John Henry Newman, one cannot help but encounter a profound unity of intellect and will, bound together by a divine call to serve. This interplay between human faculties and divine summoning echoes throughout Newman's theology, offering a compelling framework for understanding the role of the believer in the world.

Moral agency, in Newman's view, transcends mere knowledge of right and wrong. It incorporates a deeper, more substantial synthesis of intellect and will, where the knowledge of what ought to be done is seamlessly integrated with a willing disposition to act upon this knowledge. This synthesis is not an automatic or inevitable product of human nature but is the result of a participatory cooperation with divine grace. "For it is God which worketh in you both to will and to do of his good pleasure" (Phil. 2:13).

Newman's emphasis on the intellect's role in faith does not suggest an intellectualism that isolates belief within the realm of ideation and theory. Rather, he posits that true faith, while certainly engaging the intellect, necessarily compels the will towards action. This is the heart of moral agency: an intellect informed by truth and a will energized by love, manifesting in a life of service.

Such a life of service, as proposed by Newman, is not a peripheral aspect of Christian living but its very essence. The call to serve is inscribed in the fabric of baptismal grace, implicating every believer in the mission of the Church. "Let your light so shine before men, that they may see your good works, and glorify your Father which is in heaven" (Matt. 5:16). This biblical mandate underscores the intrinsic link between faith and the outward expression of that faith in acts of charity and witness.

However, Newman's understanding of moral agency does not entail a simplistic equation of action with morality. The moral agent acts not out of a mere sense of duty or obligation but from a personal, dynamic relationship with God. This relationship is cultivated through prayer, sacramental life, and an ongoing discernment of vocation, whereby the individual becomes increasingly aligned with God's will.

Furthermore, Newman highlights the uniqueness of each believer's call to serve. The diversity of gifts and talents among the faithful is not accidental but divinely ordained, intended for the common good. "But now hath God set the members every one of them in the body, as it hath pleased him" (1 Cor. 12:18). Each believer's contribution, therefore, is irreplaceable and vital to the body of Christ.

The practical implications of this theology of moral agency are far-reaching. In a world fraught with anguish and suffering, the Christian's call to serve becomes a beacon of hope and a tangible manifestation of God's love. It challenges the faithful not only to serve those within their immediate communities but to extend their service to the marginalized, the forgotten, and the vulnerable across the globe.

Moreover, Newman's vision of moral agency calls for an integration of faith and reason in addressing the ethical dilemmas of our time. By engaging the intellect in discerning the complexities of moral issues, while simultaneously heeding the will's impulse towards compassionate action, the believer becomes a genuine witness to the Gospel in the public square.

This vision, however, is not without its trials. The journey of the moral agent is marked by periods of doubt, struggle, and spiritual dryness. Yet, it is precisely in navigating these challenges that the believer's moral agency is refined and matured. "And not only so, but we glory in tribulations also: knowing that tribulation worketh patience; And patience, experience; and experience, hope" (Rom. 5:3-4).

In conclusion, Newman's theology of moral agency and the call to serve encapsulates a holistic vision of Christian discipleship. It is an invitation to a life where intellect and will, informed and transformed by faith, converge in a symphony of service. Such a life transcends the confines of personal sanctity, radiating instead as a luminous witness to the truth and love of the Gospel.

Thus, the moral agency delineated by Newman is not a static or monolithic concept but a dynamic, lived reality. It insists that faith and action, belief and practice, are inexorably linked, each informing and enriching the other. In this light, every believer is summoned not merely to an intellectual assent of faith but to a vigorous, active participation in God's redemptive work in the world.

It is here, in the fertile ground of service, that the moral agent finds the full expression of their faith. It is here that intellect and will, heaven and earth, God's grace and human endeavor, meet. And it is here that the believer, in the mystery of divine providence, becomes a co-laborer with Christ, forging a legacy of faith that transcends time and space, for "his mercy is on them that fear him from generation to generation" (Luke 1:50).

The call to serve, then, as articulated through Newman's theological vision, remains not only a fundamental aspect of Christian discipleship but its very heartbeat. In a world yearning for meaning, direction, and love, this call resounds with renewed urgency, inviting every moral agent to echo in their lives the redemptive melody of the Gospel. It is a call to action, to love, and to serve, ever mindful of the divine promise that undergirds our feeble efforts: "lo, I am with you alway, even unto the end of the world" (Matt. 28:20).

Chapter 5: The Literary Methodology of Gerard Manley Hopkins

In delving into the literary methodology of Gerard Manley Hopkins, it's essential to discern the profound underpinnings that distinguish his work from his contemporaries. Hopkins, unlike his peers, pursued a path wherein each word, rhythm, and image served as conduits to divine mystery, revealing theology not as a doctrine but as a living, breathing experience. This exploration unveils the intrinsically sacramental view of the world that Hopkins held, where every element of nature and every facet of human experience could echo the divine.

Hopkins innovated with what he termed "sprung rhythm," a poetic form that broke from the conventional metrics of his time. This rhythm, characterized by its stress on the first syllable followed by a varying number of unstressed syllables, mirrors the unpredictability and the dynamism of nature itself. Furthermore, it encapsulates the essence of divine creation, an unpredictable yet ordered beauty. This rhythm, thus, becomes a theological tool, one that Hopkins wields with precision and purpose, to draw the reader directly into the heart of an encounter with the divine, encouraging them to perceive God in all things, just as it is written, "For in him we live, and move, and have our being" (*Acts 17:28*).

The centrality of nature in Hopkins's poetry is not merely an aesthetic choice but a theological stance. Nature, in his view, is imbued with the grandeur of God, as famously captured in the line, "The world is charged with the grandeur of God" from his poem "God's Grandeur." This perspective is not pantheistic but sacramental; it understands creation as a manifestation of God's glory, a testament to the divine presence that sustains all things. Thus, when one observes the natural world through Hopkins's eyes, they are invited into a contemplation of God's immediacy and intimacy with creation.

Furthermore, Hopkins's use of imagery and alliteration in his poetry serves not only as an aesthetic device but as a means to evoke a sensory and spiritual awareness. His descriptions of nature are imbued with a deep sense of the incarnational presence of God within the physical realm. Through this vivid imagery, Hopkins bridges the divide between the sensual and the spiritual, inviting the reader to find God in the minutiae of nature and the mundane. He thus echoes the scriptural affirmation, "For the invisible things of him from the creation of the world are clearly seen, being understood by the things that are made" (*Romans 1:20*).

This sacramental vision of the world presented by Hopkins is pivotal for understanding his literary methodology. It prompts a reevaluation of the role of literature in theological reflection, suggesting that poetry, through its symbolic language and evocation of beauty, can serve as a profound medium of divine revelation. Hopkins's poetry does not merely describe the world; it serves as a lens through which the world's sacramental nature is disclosed, making tangible the grace that permeates all of creation.

In analyzing Hopkins's approach to depicting the divine in the everyday, one can't help but recognize the echo of Christ's parables. Just like these biblical stories utilized familiar elements to convey deeper truths, Hopkins employs common natural scenes to explore complex theological ideas. His work invites readers to delve deeper into their understanding of God, challenging them to see beyond the surface.

Moreover, Hopkins's personal wrestling with despair, evident in his "terrible sonnets," provides a profound exploration of faith under duress. Yet, even here, his literary approach reveals theology's power to grapple with human suffering. Hopkins does not shy away from the darkness but finds within it the potential for divine grace, an echo of the psalmist's cry, "Yea, though I walk through the valley of the shadow of death, I will fear no evil" (*Psalm 23:4*). Hopkins's work thus serves not only as a theological exploration but as a testament to the resilience of faith.

The literary methodology of Gerard Manley Hopkins stands as a testament to the transformative power of poetry, both as an art form and as a medium of theological reflection. Through his innovative use of sprung rhythm, sacramental vision of the world, and profound engagement with the divine mystery amidst suffering, Hopkins offers a compelling model for viewing literature as a vital vessel of faith. His work challenges the reader to explore the intersections of the divine and the mundane, urging a deeper contemplation of God's presence in all aspects of life.

In conclusion, the exploration of Gerard Manley Hopkins's literary methodology enriches our understanding of how literature can serve as a bridge between the human and the divine. Through his poetic innovations and deep theological insight, Hopkins invites us to contemplate the omnipresence of God in the world around us, urging us towards a deeper, more profound encounter with the sacred. His work not only contributes a unique voice to the canon of religious literature but also offers vital insights into the role of art and beauty in the spiritual journey.

In the realm of theology and literature, Hopkins's methodology emerges as a beacon, illuminating the path toward a faith that fully embraces the beauty of creation and the mystery of the divine. As such, his work remains a vital component of theological reflection, a source of inspiration for those seeking to explore the depths of faith through the lens of literature.

The Use of Sprung Rhythm as a Theological Tool

In considering the literary methodology of Gerard Manley Hopkins, it is paramount to delve into his pioneering use of sprung rhythm as a profound theological tool. This innovation not only marked his departure from conventional metrics but also served as a conduit for expressing the intricacies of divine grace and the dynamism of creation. The essence of sprung rhythm, characterized by its variegated foot and counterpointing stress patterns, mirrors the unpredictable yet harmonious nature of God's works.

At the heart of sprung rhythm lies an inherent reflection on the Creator's craftsmanship. As the poet weaves through each line, the rhythm breaks and accelerates, echoing the biblical notion that "God's ways are not our ways" (Isa. 55:8). This rhythmic flexibility allows Hopkins to craft a vivid tapestry of the divine interplay within the natural world, embodying theologically rich concepts through his poetic form.

The audacity of sprung rhythm, in its departure from the metrical norms, stands as a metaphor for the Christian's call to transcend worldly conventions. In the same way that Christ's teachings overturned societal expectations, Hopkins's poetic form invites readers into a space of spiritual reawakening. This rhythmic rebellion against the norm is not merely aesthetic but serves a higher purpose of evoking an encounter with the numinous.

Consider, for instance, the manner in which Hopkins employs this unique rhythm to explore the theme of inscape - the individual essence ordained by God for every creature and object. Through the lens of sprung rhythm, Hopkins unveils the divine signature embedded within the fabric of creation, urging a deeper contemplation on the presence of God in every detail of life.

The theological canvas of Hopkins's poetry, painted with the brush of sprung rhythm, thus becomes a vibrant manifesto of sacramentality. It is a declaration that the material world, far from being secular or profane, is imbued with divine grace, awaiting recognition and veneration. This sacramental vision, articulated through the rhythmic oscillations of his verse, challenges the reader to a renewed vision of the world as charged with the grandeur of God.

Furthermore, sprung rhythm serves as a vessel for expressing the dynamic nature of divine grace. Just as the rhythm breaks and flows, so too does grace move in the life of the believer - sometimes subtle, at other times overwhelming. Hopkins's application of this rhythm can be seen as a poetic representation of the Christian understanding of grace as a free and unmerited favor from God, fluctuating and filling the soul in accordance with divine wisdom.

The legacy of sprung rhythm, within the theological discourse, extends beyond mere literary innovation. It becomes a medium through which Hopkins communicates the ineffable mysteries of faith. In his hands, poetry transcends its form to become a lived experience of encountering the divine in the mundane. His work invites a contemplation that is not only intellectual but deeply spiritual, offering glimpses into the mystery of the divine made manifest in the world.

In the contemplation of beauty, a central theme to Hopkins's theology articulated through sprung rhythm, one perceives a reflection of the Creator's beauty. "Beauty is truth, truth beauty," as the adage goes, finds resonance in this context, wherein the aesthetic experience of Hopkins's poetry becomes an encounter with divine truth.

The interaction between sprung rhythm and theological content in Hopkins's poetry thus mirrors the biblical relationship between the word and the Spirit. As the scriptures state, "In the beginning was the Word, and the Word was with God, and the Word was God" (John 1:1). Hopkins's poetic form, in its vitality and innovation, embodies this Word, dynamically alive and infused with the Spirit's breath.

In exploring the depths of human suffering and divine sorrow, Hopkins employs sprung rhythm to articulate the profound mystery of the Paschal mystery. The tension and release inherent in the rhythm reflect the

Christian narrative of death and resurrection, encapsulating the hope and despair intertwined in the human condition.

This rhythmic structure, with its capacity for sudden shifts and emotional depth, allows Hopkins to navigate the paradoxes of faith. In his verse, the coexistence of joy and sorrow, beauty and decay, speaks to the complexity of the Christian journey, marked by the cross yet suffused with the light of resurrection.

It is within this unique rhythmic framework that Hopkins's poetry articulates a compelling theological anthropology. It suggests an understanding of humanity as inherently rhythmic beings, created to live in harmony with the divine cadence. Sprung rhythm, therefore, becomes a metaphor for the human soul's alignment with God's will - a dance of synchronicity with the Creator.

In conclusion, the use of sprung rhythm by Gerard Manley Hopkins transcends mere literary technique; it is a theological tool of profound depth. Through its innovation, Hopkins not only revolutionized English poetry but also offered a new lens through which to experience and contemplate the divine. His work, rooted in this unique rhythmic form, continues to inspire and challenge, beckoning to a deeper engagement with the mysteries of faith, nature, and the human spirit.

Thus, sprung rhythm, in the hands of Hopkins, becomes not just a method of conveying theological truths but an active participant in the divine drama of creation, redemption, and revelation. It invites the reader to an encounter with the living God, through the medium of poetic beauty and rhythmic grace, opening new vistas of understanding and devotion.

Nature and the Divine: Hopkins' Perspective

In the meticulous and profound oeuvre of Gerard Manley Hopkins, one witnesses a resonant interplay between the natural world and the divine. His writings, deeply imbued with theological contemplation, present nature not merely as a backdrop to human activity but as a vibrant, animated participant in the divine dance. This perspective, distinct yet harmonically aligned with biblical teachings, offers a rich terrain for exploration.

Hopkins saw in nature an inexhaustible source of divine revelation. "The world is charged with the grandeur of God," he famously begins in "God's Grandeur," invoking a sense of the Almighty's presence permeating through creation. This encapsulation offers an insight into Hopkins' theological vision, where nature is a conduit of God's presence, a theme that aligns with "For the invisible things of him from the creation of the world are clearly seen, being understood by the things that are made, even his eternal power and Godhead" (Rom. 1:20).

However, Hopkins went beyond merely acknowledging nature's beauty. He saw in it a reflection of Christ's own incarnation, suffering, and resurrection. In his poetic imagination, the natural cycle of growth, decay, and renewal became a powerful metaphor for Christ's passion and redemption of the world. This perspective is imbued with the idea that all creation participates in the salvific narrative, an interpretation that draws us closer to the mystery of God's continuous act of creation and redemption.

Moreover, Hopkins' employment of sprung rhythm in his poetry imitates the unpredictability and vibrancy of nature itself. Just as no two branches grow in the same manner, his verses follow an organic pattern, mirroring the uniqueness of God's creation. This distinct rhythm, coupled with Hopkins' use of inscape and instress, provides a literary methodology through which the poet seeks to capture the essence of each creature's unique relationship with its creator.

It's pivotal to grasp Hopkins' concept of 'inscape,' the individual essence or form unique to every created thing, as an expression of God's infinite creativity. Each creature, each landscape holds within it a particular reflection of God's face. Consequently, by striving to articulate these inscapes, Hopkins' work invites us to gaze more intently, to recognize and reverence the divine fingerprints on every aspect of the natural world.

Similarly, 'instress,' the energetic force that sustains the inscape, becomes in Hopkins' theology a metaphor for the sustaining word of God that upholds all things. "By the word of the Lord were the heavens made; and all the host of them by the breath of his mouth" (Ps. 33:6). In this light, Hopkins doesn't just see nature; he witnesses the ongoing, dynamic act of creation, a testament to God's perpetual presence and action in the world.

His contemplation of nature, therefore, evolves into a form of worship, a way to acknowledge and praise the Creator. For Hopkins, to study the natural world — to truly see it — is an act of reverence, a participation in the divine liturgy that the universe ceaselessly offers to its Creator. "Are not two sparrows sold for a farthing? and one of them shall not fall on the ground without your Father" (Matt. 10:29). Even in the smallest creature, Hopkins perceives a reflection of God's care and attention.

Furthermore, Hopkins' environmental sensibility anticipates modern ecological concerns. He perceived the despoliation of the earth not merely as an aesthetic loss but as a spiritual affront, a disruption of the harmonious order that God intended for creation. His lamentation over the felling of the Binsey Poplars reveals a heart grieved by man's failure to recognize and respect the sanctity of God's creation, echoing the biblical mandate to steward the earth responsibly.

Yet, Hopkins' perspective on nature was not naively romantic. He was acutely aware of the brutality and indifference present in the natural world, characteristics that seemingly stand in contrast to the notion of a loving, providential Creator. This tension, however, did not lead him to despair but rather deepened his faith, as he perceived in the struggle and suffering of creation a participation in the paschal mystery. Like Christ's own foreseeable resurrection through His suffering, nature's cycle of death and rebirth stood as a testament to Hopkins' belief in the ultimate triumph of God's grace and glory through adversity.

In poems like "Pied Beauty," Hopkins celebrates the "dappled things" of the world, the variegated beauty that reflects God's delight in diversity. He encourages an attitude of gratitude for the "original, spare, strange" aspects of creation, urging a recognition of beauty in places where it might not be conventionally sought. This attitude parallels the biblical exhortation to "give thanks in all circumstances; for this is God's will for you in Christ Jesus" (1 Thess. 5:18).

In Hopkins, then, we find not just a poet but a profoundly spiritual theologian, one for whom the natural world and its relationship with the divine serves as a central locus of contemplation and revelation. His writings challenge us to look beyond the superficial, to perceive in every leaf and stone, every creature great and small, the indelible signature of the Creator.

Through his innovative poetic form and his deeply incarnational theology, Hopkins crafts a vision of the world imbued with divinity, a sacramental cosmos where matter and spirit are intimately intertwined. His work invites us into a deeper engagement with the world, to a space where faith and imagination, theology and poetry, the natural and the supernatural, converge in a profound and life-affirming synthesis.

Therefore, as followers of Christ and admirers of Hopkins' literary methodology, we are called not simply to witness but to participate in the ongoing dialogue between creation and Creator, to recognize and cherish the divine narrative inscribed in the natural world. The challenge Hopkins presents is one of attentiveness and awe, a summons to behold with new eyes the "dearest freshness deep down things" as evidence of a God who is ever-present, ever-creative, ever-inviting us into a deeper communion with Him and with all He has made.

In concluding this exploration of Hopkins' perspective on nature and the divine, one comes away with a renewed sense of wonder and responsibility towards the created order. Hopkins teaches us that every element of nature is a theophany, a manifestation of God, calling us to a deeper faith, a greater reverence, and a more profound commitment to preserving the integrity and harmony of God's creation. His poetic voice, a blend of fervent faith and keen observation, continues to echo, urging us to see in nature not only the grandeur of God but also our own place within the divine narrative, as stewards of the Earth and participants in the ongoing work of redemption.

Chapter 6: Contrasting Views on Sin and Redemption

In the theological landscape where sin's shadow looms large, redemption's light shines all the brighter, offering a path from the depths of despair to the heights of grace. This duality of human nature and divine mercy serves as a foundational concept within the works of many theologians and writers, among whom John Henry Newman and Gerard Manley Hopkins stand out. Both grapple with the heavy burden of sin, yet their approaches to understanding and overcoming it illuminate the nuanced ways in which faith can intersect with personal narrative and theological doctrine. Newman, with his keen insight into the human condition, perceives sin not merely as an act of moral failure but as a profound disorientation of the soul from its divine origin and purpose *(Rom. 3:23)*.

Contrastingly, Hopkins, with his poetic sensibility, witnesses sin as a dark foil to the overwhelming beauty of God's grace. Where Newman articulates the consequences of sin through a lens that emphasizes separation from God, Hopkins finds in the same darkness a canvas for the light of grace to shine most brilliantly. For Hopkins, God's grace is not merely a counter to sin, but an active force that beautifies and transforms, turning even the darkest night into a prelude for dawn *(Ps. 30:5)*. His poetic works, rich in imagery and rhythm, convey not only the struggle against sin but the transformative power of grace, the beauty of which is made all the more poignant against the backdrop of human frailty.

The contrasting views of Newman and Hopkins on sin and redemption delve into the heart of Christian theology, each offering a unique lens through which the divine drama of redemption unfolds. Where Newman provides a roadmap of returning to God through the recognition of sin's consequences and the necessity of divine mercy, Hopkins celebrates redemption as an ongoing process of renewal and beauty. Both paths, though distinct, converge on the essential truth that redemption is not merely a singular moment of salvific grace but a continual journey of turning away from sin and towards the light of God's love *(1 John 1:7)*. Through their respective works, Newman and Hopkins invite us into a deeper understanding of sin and redemption, challenging us to see beyond the scars of sin to the beauty of grace that lies beyond.

Newman's Approach to Sin and Its Consequences

In the discourse of faith and reason, John Henry Newman stands as a beacon, illuminating the harsh realities and consequences of sin through a lens that combines the cogency of intellect with the profundity of divine revelation. This section probes deeply into Newman's contemplations on sin and its repercussions, unpacking a narrative where literature and theology converge in a harmonious exposition. It's a discourse where sin isn't merely an abstract concept but a palpable force with tangible repercussions on the human spirit and its relationship with the Divine.

At the core of Newman's reflection is the understanding that sin is more than an act; it's a state that ensnares the human soul, distancing it from God. "For all have sinned, and come short of the glory of God;" (Rom. 3:23) isn't just a biblical verse to Newman; it's a fundamental truth that underscores the human predicament. In this light, sin is not just personal failure but a cosmic fracture that affects our innate connection with the Creator.

Newman discerns the gravity of sin not only in its action but in its consequence. The wages of sin, as scripture attests, "is death" (Rom. 6:23), not solely in the physical demise but in the spiritual separation from God, the source of all life. This separation creates a chasm, a spiritual void that can't be bridged by human efforts alone. Newman's theology hence underscores the necessity of divine grace for redemption, a grace that is both unmerited and freely given.

However, Newman doesn't leave the sinner in despair. In his approach, the recognition of sin becomes the first step towards reconciliation with God. It's in acknowledging our brokenness that the path to healing and redemption is unveiled. Just as a physician can't treat a patient who denies his illness, so too is the soul that doesn't recognize its sinful state barred from the grace that heals.

For Newman, sin also carries with it societal consequences. He perceives sin not just as individual moral failures but as collective actions that degrade and debase society. In this view, sin is like a contagion that spreads, affecting not just the sinner but the community at large. It's a ripple that disturbs the societal fabric, challenging the notion of communal harmony and the common good.

The sacrament of confession, in Newman's eyes, serves as a divine remedy to the malady of sin. It's in the act of confessing that the sinner unburdens the soul, opening up to the transforming power of God's mercy. Confession is thus portrayed as a sacramental encounter where divine grace meets human frailty, a nexus where forgiveness and healing are dispensed.

Newman's theology is steeped in the concept of contrition, a heartfelt sorrow for sins committed combined with the resolve to amend one's ways. This contrition is not superficial but emanates from a profound realization of the offense against divine love. "Create in me a clean heart, O God; and renew a right spirit within me." (Ps. 51:10) encapsulates the essence of Newman's call to contrition, a call to return to the purity of heart that mirrors God's own holiness.

The interplay of sin and grace in Newman's theology is a testament to the dynamic nature of the Christian faith, a journey that navigates through the valleys of sin towards the peaks of grace. It's a pilgrimage marked by moments of faltering and falling, yet always buoyed by the hope of divine mercy. Newman sees in this pilgrimage the transformative power of grace, a force capable of renewing the human heart and restoring it to its original dignity.

In the fabric of Newman's thought, the church plays a pivotal role as the custodian of grace. It's within the bosom of the church that the sinner finds refuge and renewal. The church, with its sacraments, serves as the conduit of divine grace, the ark that carries the faithful across the turbulent waters of sin towards the shore of salvation.

Newman's reflections on sin and its consequences aren't merely theological assertions but are imbued with a profound literary quality. His writings are a tapestry where philosophical insights and theological principles are woven with the threads of eloquence and literary grace. It's in this literary craftsmanship that Newman's approach to sin and redemption resonates not just with the intellect but with the soul, inviting a contemplative engagement with the mysteries of faith.

In concluding, Newman's approach to sin and its consequences serves as a beacon, guiding the faithful through the tumultuous seas of human frailty. It's an approach that doesn't shy away from confronting the darkness of sin but does so with a hopeful gaze towards the horizon of grace. By integrating the richness of literature with the depth of theology, Newman's reflections offer a pathway that leads from the acknowledgment of sin to the embrace of divine forgiveness, a journey from darkness into the marvelous light of redemption.

The narrative of sin and redemption, as articulated by Newman, thus becomes a symphony of hope, a testament to the power of grace to overcome the chasm of sin. It's a narrative that invites the faithful to embark on a journey of transformation, a journey that leads to the fullness of life in God. In Newman's approach, we find not just a theology of sin and its consequences but an invitation to experience the profound love of God that calls each soul from the shadows of sin into the glory of His grace.

To dwell on Newman's insights is to embark upon a journey that traverses the depths of human weakness and the heights of divine mercy. It's a journey that challenges and comforts, that convicts and consoles. Through his literary genius and theological acumen, Newman maps out a pathway that leads towards the heart of the Christian mystery - the redemption of the sinner by the boundless grace of God.

Hopkins and the Beauty of Grace

The notion of grace, as a divine assistance given to humans for their regeneration and sanctification, pervades the theological and literary works of Gerard Manley Hopkins. Unique in his perception, Hopkins envisioned grace not merely as a theological concept but as a palpable presence that imbued the natural world and human experience with divine beauty. Through his innovative poetics and profound spirituality, Hopkins offers a vivid exploration of grace's transformative power, contrasting sharply with more traditional views of sin and redemption.

In the landscape of Christian doctrine, grace occupies a central position, serving as the bridge between human frailty and divine redemption. Hopkins, however, perceived grace as more than a doctrinal cornerstone; he saw it as the very lifeblood of creation, a force that dances within the confines of the natural and the spiritual realms alike. "The world is charged with the grandeur of God," he famously declares in "God's Grandeur," suggesting an omnipresence of grace that charges the mundane with divine significance (Hopkins, 1877).

This electrifying presence of the divine in the mundane is a hallmark of Hopkins's work, showcasing his belief in a God who is deeply immanent in His creation. Unlike approaches that view grace as a distant, abstract gift bestowed by a remote deity, Hopkins's poetry pulsates with the immediacy of God's grace, transforming the way we perceive the world around us. It prompts a shift from seeing grace as a mere antidote to sin, to viewing it as the very substrate that nurtures the soul's growth towards God.

In the analysis of sin and redemption, Hopkins's focus on grace introduces a radical optimism. Where sin is often portrayed as a chasm separating humanity from God, Hopkins's writings shimmer with the conviction that grace is ever-present, patiently waiting to transmute our basest instincts into reflections of divine love. This perspective is deeply rooted in Hopkins's Jesuit spirituality, which emphasizes God's unending mercy and the possibility of renewal through grace.

Consider "The Windhover", where Hopkins marvels at the majesty of a bird in flight, seeing in its mastery of the air a metaphor for the grace-empowered soul that rises above sin and temptation. The poem isn't just an ode to natural beauty, but a testament to Hopkins's belief in the human capacity to participate in divine grace, to transcend the mundane through the recognition of God's omnipresence.

Yet, Hopkins was no stranger to darkness. His "Terrible Sonnets" reveal a soul grappling with despair and the seeming absence of God's grace. However, even here, grace is not absent but hidden; a latent force that awaits acknowledgment even in the depths of spiritual desolation. Hopkins's struggle underscores a profound truth: grace requires our cooperation, our assent to let it work within and through us, even when its presence is not immediately felt.

This concept of cooperative grace suggests a partnership between the divine and the human, where grace acts not as a unilateral imposition, but as an invitation to engage in the divine life. It's a dynamic process where the human response to grace becomes as crucial as the grace itself. Hopkins's poetry encapsulates this participatory understanding of grace, portraying it as an ongoing dialogue between God and creation.

In exploring the theme of redemption, Hopkins diverges from the notion of grace as a simple remedy to sin, proposing instead that grace is transformative and creative. It does not just restore us to our original state but elevates us, enabling us to reflect God's beauty in unique ways. This transformative power of grace is apparent in his use of sprung rhythm and innovative metrics, which break conventional poetic forms to reveal new dimensions of beauty, mirroring how grace works in the human soul.

Hopkins's poetic form itself becomes a metaphor for grace's action: just as his verse transcends traditional structures, so does grace transcend and transform the limitations of our fallen nature. In Hopkins's view, grace ennobles and beautifies, making our souls a "fresco" of divine artistry. This understanding elevates the discourse on sin and redemption from a legalistic framework to an aesthetic and deeply personal experience of divine love.

This aesthetic aspect of grace in Hopkins's theology reflects a sacramental view of the world, where tangible elements of creation become conduits of divine grace. Every leaf, bird, or wave serves not only as a sign of God's grandeur but as an active participant in the divine economy of salvation. This sacramental vision bridges the gap between the spiritual and the material, inviting believers to encounter grace in the ordinary, in the tangible.

Hopkins's treatment of grace sheds light on the potential for beauty and transformation inherent in every aspect of creation, including human struggles and failings. It proposes that grace works not by circumventing nature or humanity's flawed condition but by penetrating and perfecting them from within. Thus, redemption, in Hopkins's view, is not an escape from the world but a sanctification of it, achieved through the recognition and embrace of grace in all things.

The poet's intense personal experiences of both grace and desolation enrich his theological insights, lending them a credibility born of lived experience. Hopkins did not simply theorize about grace; he encountered it, wrestled with it, and strove to express its beauty and complexity through his poetry. His work stands as a testament to the power of artistic expression in navigating and illuminating the mysteries of faith.

In "Pied Beauty," Hopkins calls for praise of God's diverse creation, highlighting the splendor of "dappled things." This celebration of diversity and imperfection as sources of beauty offers a refreshing counter-narrative to overly simplistic notions of sin and grace. Hopkins suggests that grace infuses even the most irregular aspects of creation, inviting a reevaluation of what it means to be redeemed and sanctified.

In conclusion, Hopkins's understanding of grace as a transformative, aesthetic, and omnipresent force offers a profound counterpoint to traditional narratives of sin and redemption. His work urges us to see grace not as a distant, abstract doctrine, but as a vital, beautiful reality that permeates every aspect of our existence. In Hopkins's poetry, we find an invitation to view the world, and our place within it, through the lens of divine grace, recognizing in every moment and every creature the potential for redemption and sanctity.

The beauty of grace, as articulated by Hopkins, reminds us that redemption is an ongoing process of becoming, a journey marked by moments of revelation, struggle, and ultimately, transformation. It's a journey that reflects the broader quest for meaning and connection in a world brimming with God's presence, waiting to be acknowledged and celebrated. In embracing this vision, we open ourselves to the boundless possibilities of grace, finding in our encounters with the divine an inexhaustible source of inspiration, hope, and beauty.

Chapter 7: The Moral Obligations of the Christian Intellectual

In the lives of those dedicated to the pursuit of both intellectual and spiritual excellence, the intertwining paths of faith and reason are not merely coincidental but are divinely ordained. The moral obligations of the Christian intellectual, a vocation both noble and demanding, are deeply rooted in the scriptural calling to use one's talents for the greater glory of God. As the parable of the talents teaches, "His lord said unto him, Well done, thou good and faithful servant: thou hast been faithful over a few things, I will make thee ruler over many things: enter thou into the joy of thy lord" (Matt. 25:21). This biblical injunction underscores the imperative for intellectuals gifted in the arenas of literature and theology to employ their unique aptitudes not as ends in themselves but as means toward the ultimate end of evangelization and moral uplift.

The Christian intellectual is thus charged with a twofold mission: to seek the truth unceasingly through the rigors of reason and intellect, and to bear witness to that truth through a steadfast commitment to moral and ethical principles as revealed in the Gospels. It is not sufficient to dwell in the ivory tower of abstract thought; one must descend into the arena of human experience, where the Word becomes flesh, living out the precepts of faith in daily action. Just as salt loses its flavor if kept within a saltshaker, so too do the talents of the Christian intellectual risk becoming futile if not exercised within the reality of the human condition. "Ye are the salt of the earth... Ye are the light of the world. A city that is set on a hill cannot be hid" (Matt. 5:13-14). In echoing Christ's words, the imperative resounds for those endowed with intellectual and literary gifts to illuminate the moral and spiritual darkness of the world.

To this end, the roles of John Henry Newman and Gerard Manley Hopkins serve as exemplary archetypes of how the fusion of intellect and spirituality can germinate within the heart of the society the seeds of a profound moral and theological revival. By weaving together the threads of their theological insights with the fabric of their literary genius, they underscored the sacramentality of everyday life, affirming the presence of divine grace in the minutiae of human experience. Their lives and works attest to the reality that the Christian intellectual is called not only to ascend the heights of intellectual achievement but also to transfigure the world through the leaven of their moral and spiritual leadership. The call to transform society through the gifts of intellect and faith thus remains ever urgent, beckoning future generations of Christian scholars to tread the path first blazed by these luminous figures.

Newman's View on the Use of Talents for God's Service

In the landscape of Christian thought, the stewardship of talents emerges as a paramount responsibility bestowed upon the faithful. This stewardship, a divine trust, encompasses the cultivation and deployment of one's gifts for the greater glory of God. Within this framework, John Henry Newman's perspective on the utilization of talents for divine service offers profound insights into the moral obligations of the Christian intellectual. Through an examination of Newman's theology, a rich understanding of the role of talents in the service of God and community can be gleaned.

Newman, in his contemplations, posits that every individual is endowed with unique talents by the Creator. This endowment, however, is not a matter of personal prerogative but a sacred charge, "For unto whomsoever much is given, of him shall be much required" (Luke 12:48). It thus becomes a Christian's duty not only to cultivate these talents but to deploy them in manners that align with God's will, illuminating paths of truth, beauty, and goodness in the world.

Central to Newman's discourse on talents is the idea that the intellect, when consecrated to God's service, becomes a powerful instrument for the advancement of the Kingdom of God on earth. Intellectual pursuits, therefore, are not to be seen as ends in themselves but as means to a far greater purpose: the illumination of the divine truth in a world marred by skepticism and disbelief.

The apt application of one's talents, according to Newman, involves a discerning engagement with contemporary culture and scholarship. The Christian intellectual is thus called to navigate the complex waters of modern thought, engaging critically yet constructively, ensuring that the light of Christ is not obscured but shines forth, "that they may see your good works, and glorify your Father which is in heaven" (Matt. 5:16).

Further, Newman emphasizes the importance of humility in the service of one's talents. It is a recognition that all gifts, no matter their magnitude, originate from the same divine source, and their purpose is to serve that source's ends. This humility fosters a spirit of generosity and openness, essential for the fruitful collaboration in God's service.

The transformative potential of talents used in God's service is a recurrent theme in Newman's theology. This transformation occurs not only within the individual employing their gifts in accordance with divine will but also within the broader community that benefits from such service. The Christian intellectual, through their dedicated service, becomes a beacon of hope and a catalyst for change, reflecting the transformative power of the Gospel.

In practice, Newman's view advocates for an integrated approach to talent use, where spiritual, intellectual, and social dimensions inform and enhance one another. This holistic engagement ensures that talents are not developed or used in a vacuum but contribute to the building up of the Church and society.

Moreover, Newman's perspective acknowledges the challenges and sacrifices involved in the faithful use of talents. It demands a steadfast commitment to truth and righteousness, often in the face of opposition or indifference. Yet, it is precisely in these challenges that the depth of one's faith and the authenticity of one's dedication are tested and proven.

Recognition of one's talents as gifts for God's service also fosters a profound sense of purpose and direction in life. Newman suggests that understanding and embracing this purpose can lead to a deeper fulfillment and joy than any worldly success can offer. This fulfillment stems from the knowledge that one is participating in God's salvific work in the world.

For Newman, then, the use of talents in God's service is an integral aspect of Christian witness in the contemporary world. It is through the faithful stewardship of these gifts that Christians can most effectively testify to the truth, beauty, and goodness of the Gospel, inviting others to encounter the living God.

In conclusion, Newman's insights into the use of talents for God's service present a compelling vision for the Christian intellectual. This vision combines a deep reverence for God's gifts, an active engagement with contemporary thought, and a dedicated service to the community. It challenges believers to view their talents not merely as personal assets but as sacred trusts to be used in fulfillment of their divine calling.

The stewardship of talents, as articulated by Newman, calls for a balance between self-development and self-giving, urging Christians to cultivate their gifts while remaining ever mindful of the ultimate purpose of such endeavors: the glory of God and the advancement of His Kingdom. In embracing this call, the Christian intellectual finds not only the path to personal sanctification but also the means to contribute to the sanctification of the world.

Finally, in reflecting on Newman's view, one is reminded of the timeless relevance of his thought for contemporary Christians. In an age characterized by myriad challenges and opportunities, the faithful application of talents in God's service remains a potent force for good, capable of transforming lives and societies. It is a testament to the enduring power of Christian commitment and the transformative potential of lives lived in accordance with divine will.

Hopkins: The Sacramentality of Everyday Life

Within the vibrant framework of Christian philosophy, Gerard Manley Hopkins' exploration of the sacramentality of everyday life emerges as a profound testament to the connection between the divine and the mundane. His perspective illuminates the path for intellectuals and believers alike, urging them to recognize the presence of God in all aspects of life, from the grandest landscapes to the simplest of pleasures. Hopkins' vision, deeply rooted in his Catholic faith, challenges the conventional separation between sacred and secular, suggesting a world teeming with divine presence, where every element of creation reflects the Creator's grandeur.

At the heart of Hopkins' theology lies the conviction that the natural world is charged with the grandeur of God, as articulated in his famous sonnet. This belief extends beyond the appreciation of nature's beauty to encompass a deeper, sacramental understanding of reality. In Hopkins' view, the material world is not merely a backdrop to the spiritual life but is integral to it, serving as a conduit through which the divine communicates with humanity. For him, the world is a canvas painted by God, each brushstroke imbued with significance, awaiting the discerning eye of faith to uncover its hidden messages.

The sacramentality of everyday life, according to Hopkins, obliges the Christian intellectual to adopt a stance of constant wonder and contemplation. In this mode of being, the mundane transforms into the extraordinary, revealing glimpses of divine truth. This approach demands a radical attentiveness to the world, an openness to encountering God in all things, and an acknowledgment of His presence in the least expected places.

This perspective significantly impacts the moral obligations of the Christian intellectual. It calls for a reorientation of priorities, with an emphasis on perceiving and responding to God's presence in the world. Such a stance necessitates a commitment to stewardship, fostering care for creation as an expression of love for the Creator. Moreover, it impels the intellectual to view their talents as gifts to be employed in articulating and highlighting the sacred in the secular, to bridge the gap between the divine and the everyday.

Hopkins' poetry serves as a prime example of this sacramental vision in action. Through his innovative use of language and meter, Hopkins crafts verses that evoke the immediate presence of God in nature and human experience. His work is not merely an artistic endeavor but a mode of theological expression, an attempt to capture the ineffable in words. The Christian intellectual, following Hopkins' example, is thus called to a creative engagement with the world, employing their scholarly and artistic talents to unveil the hidden sacramentality of ordinary life.

The ethical implications of Hopkins' sacramentality extend into the social realm as well. Recognizing the divine imprint in every individual challenges prevailing attitudes of indifference and injustice. It demands a radical hospitality and generosity, grounded in the recognition of each person's inherent dignity as a reflection of the divine image. For the Christian intellectual, this translates into an advocacy for justice and a commitment to serving the marginalized, seeing in their faces the face of Christ.

Furthermore, Hopkins' sacramentality enriches one's understanding of liturgy and worship. It blurs the lines between the church's formal sacraments and the "sacraments" encountered in daily life, suggesting a continuity between liturgical celebration and everyday experiences of grace. This insight invites the believer to approach each moment with a liturgical heart, seeing time itself as a sacred offering to God.

In embracing the sacramentality of everyday life, the Christian intellectual finds not only a pathway to deeper communion with the divine but also a source of resilience and hope. In a world often marked by despair and disconnection, Hopkins' vision offers a reminder of the relentless presence of grace, imperceptibly woven into the fabric of our days. It reassures us that no aspect of life is too mundane to be touched by the divine, encouraging a posture of gratitude and awe.

The call to recognize and celebrate the sacramentality of everyday life comes with its challenges. It requires a disciplined attentiveness, a readiness to encounter the divine in the ordinary, and a willingness to let this recognition transform one's way of being in the world. For Hopkins, this was a path fraught with personal trials yet illuminated by moments of transcendent beauty and profound connection with God.

In conclusion, Hopkins' elucidation of the sacramentality of everyday life serves as a clarion call to the Christian intellectual. It beckons them to embark on a journey of discovery, to look with fresh eyes upon the world, and to see in its ordinariness the extraordinary workings of the divine. Through this sacramental lens, every aspect of life becomes an opportunity for encounter with God, transforming the intellectual's moral landscape and impelling them toward a life of service, contemplation, and praise. In embodying this vision, the Christian intellectual not only deepens their own faith but becomes a beacon of God's presence in the world, guiding others to see and savor the divine in the details of daily life.

"For in him we live, and move, and have our being; as certain also of your own poets have said, For we are also his offspring." (Acts 17:28). Hopkins, in his life and work, exemplified this scriptural truth, living out the conviction that all of creation is indeed a testament to the boundless love and creativity of God. It is this recognition of the sacramentality of everyday life that offers a fertile ground for the moral and intellectual endeavors of the Christian faithful, charting a course toward a more profound engagement with the mystery of existence and the endless possibilities for encountering the divine in the here and now.

Chapter 8: Evangelization Through Art and Literature

In this chapter, we delve deep into the crucial role art and literature play in the evangelization of the faith, examining the profound contributions of notable figures who used their creative talents as a conduit for divine truth. It is within the pages of their works and the strokes of their art that we discover an invigorating avenue for propagating the Gospel. "Let your light so shine before men, that they may see your good works, and glorify your Father which is in heaven" (Matt. 5:16). This Biblically ordained mandate serves as the foundational premise for our exploration into how creativity acts as a beacon of God's truth.

Art and literature possess an inherently persuasive power, capable of stirring souls and awakening a deeper spiritual sensibility. Through narratives that captivate and imagery that speaks volumes beyond the confines of language, creative minds have long been instrumental in leading hearts towards the divine. It is through the masterful weaving of words and the poignant capture of the visual that a bridge is built between the earthly and the ethereal, enabling a communion of the human spirit with transcendental truths.

Among those who harnessed this power with profound efficacy were Newman and Hopkins, each in their unique way illustrating the potential of creative expression as a medium for evangelization. Newman, with his eloquent prose and insightful essays, provided a reasoned and compelling case for the truths of faith, appealing to the intellect while touching the heart. Hopkins, on the other hand, captured the imagination and invoked a sense of wonder through his innovative poetry, revealing the presence of God in the natural world and the depth of His grace in the human experience. Both men demonstrated that art and literature are not mere entertainment but are vessels of profound spiritual insight and catalysts for conversion.

The beauty inherent in these works of art and literature serves not only as a reflection of the divine beauty but as an invitation to delve deeper into the mysteries of faith. As both Newman and Hopkins exemplified, creative endeavors imbued with truth and beauty have the capacity to guide souls toward a deeper understanding and appreciation of God. This evangelization through art and literature is a testament to the power of beauty to move hearts, transform minds, and draw individuals closer to the divine. It is in the embrace of these creative expressions that one finds a path to seeing the world anew, infused with the presence of the Creator.

Ultimately, the evangelization through art and literature underscores the indelible link between the aesthetic and the spiritual, affirming that the pursuit of beauty in our creative expressions is a noble and effective means of drawing closer to God. As we continue to explore the impact of Newman and Hopkins on faith and literature, we are reminded of the profound capability of art to serve as a beacon of God's truth and love. In embracing our talents and creative inclinations, we participate in the evangelization of the world, illuminating the divine truth in a manner that resonates deeply within the human heart.

Newman's Literary Evangelism

The endeavor to communicate the divine through the written word stands as a testimony to the conviction that art and literature bear a unique form of apostolic zeal. It is within this spirit that one observes the literary evangelism of John Henry Newman, whose oeuvre not only sought to elucidate theological truths but also to kindle a transformative encounter with the divine. Newman's conviction, that the pursuit of truth through beauty and narrative could uplift the soul towards the transcendent, serves as a cornerstone in understanding his approach to evangelization.

In the tapestry of Newman's literary contributions, one discerns a palpable intention to engage the intellect and will of the reader. It's an exercise that transcends mere intellectual assent to encompass the full embrace of faith through the aesthetic realm. "Let your light so shine before men, that they may see your good works, and glorify your Father which is in heaven" (Matt. 5:16). This scriptural invocation mirrors Newman's literary method, where the illumination of truth through literature serves not merely to instruct but to inspire a deeper conversion of heart.

The symbiosis of art and evangelization in Newman's corpus is most evident in his sermons and novels, where narrative and prose work conjointly to unveil the divine. His sermons, rich in imagery and imbued with profound theological insights, serve as a form of literary evangelism that appeals directly to the soul's yearning for beauty and truth. Herein, Newman's craftsmanship transcends the pulpit to become a literary beacon, guiding the faithful towards a deeper comprehension and appreciation of their faith.

Moreover, Newman's novel "Loss and Gain" provides a narrative framework through which the journey of faith is explored. The novel's protagonist, through various trials and tribulations, gradually moves towards the Catholic faith, embodying Newman's own journey of conversion. This literary depiction of faith's complexity and the personal quest for truth underscores Newman's evangelistic strategy: to mirror the intricate process of conversion, demonstrating that faith is both a personal and communal pilgrimage towards God.

In deploying literature as a means of evangelization, Newman understood the profundity of storytelling as a vehicle for conveying theological and moral truths. It's in the narratives of joy, suffering, doubt, and redemption that the reader encounters the lived experience of faith, making abstract theological concepts tangible and relatable. Newman's stories are imbued with an incarnational theology, embodying the Word in the flesh of characters and plots, making visible the invisible grace at work in the world.

This incarnational aspect of Newman's literature reveals an underlying principle in his evangelism: the recognition of God's presence in the mundane and the extraordinary. Through his writings, Newman invites readers to perceive the sacramental nature of reality, where divine grace suffuses all things. Literature, for Newman, becomes a sacrament in its own right—a visible sign of an invisible grace, capable of mediating a real encounter with God.

Furthermore, Newman's literary works are steeped in a profound sense of moral urgency, reflecting his belief in the transformative power of art and literature. Through the moral dilemmas and spiritual journeys of his characters, Newman foregrounds the essential role of conscience and moral discernment in the Christian life. His narratives serve as a clarion call to live a life of virtue, integrity, and holiness, echoing the Pauline exhortation to "put on the new man, which after God is created in righteousness and true holiness" (Eph. 4:24).

It is within this rich soil of Newman's literary and theological imagination that one discovers the fruits of his literary evangelism. His contributions extend beyond the confines of academia and the church, reaching into the hearts of those who seek, those who doubt, and those who yearn for a deeper relationship with the divine. Newman's literary corpus, framed by an unwavering commitment to truth and beauty, serves as a beacon that guides the reader towards the luminous mystery of God.

In contemplating the scope and impact of Newman's literary evangelism, one must not overlook the contextual backdrop against which his works were written. In an era marked by rapid social and intellectual changes, Newman's literature offered a poignant response to the emerging challenges of secularism and skepticism. Through his novels, sermons, and essays, Newman engaged with the pressing issues of his time, providing a voice of hope and a path to faith amidst the tumult of the 19th century.

The legacy of Newman's literary evangelism lies not merely in the aesthetic beauty or intellectual rigor of his works but in their capacity to transform hearts and minds. As a testament to the enduring power of literature to convey the divine, Newman's oeuvre invites us to reflect on the role of art and narrative in our own journey of faith. It challenges us to consider how we, too, can use our talents and creativity in the service of God's kingdom, echoing the evangelistic zeal that animated Newman's literary pursuits.

In conclusion, Newman's integration of art and literature into the fabric of evangelization represents a multifaceted approach to witnessing the faith. His literary corpus, permeated with theological depth and aesthetic sensitivity, stands as an enduring testament to the potential of the written word to awaken the soul to the beauty of the divine. In a world increasingly marked by fragmentation and secularization, Newman's literary evangelism continues to offer a beacon of hope, beckoning us to encounter the divine Word through the beauty of human words.

Thus, the examination of Newman's literary evangelism not only enriches our understanding of his theological vision but also inspires us to reconceive our approach to evangelization in the modern world. By weaving together the threads of art, literature, and theology, we can cultivate a more holistic and engaging form of witness—a witness that resonates with the complexity and beauty of the human experience in its quest for the divine.

Hopkins and the Witness of Beauty

In the vast ocean where art and faith converge, Gerard Manley Hopkins stands as a beacon, a testament to the transformative power of beauty in leading souls to the Divine. His poetry, rich in imagery and dense with theological undertones, serves not merely as a body of literary work but as a salient call to witness the omnipresence of God through the lens of aesthetic wonder. This chapter aims to delve into Hopkins' unique ability to use beauty as a medium for evangelization, aligning closely with the belief that art, in its highest form, is a conduit to the divine.

The psalmist sang, "O Lord, how manifold are thy works! in wisdom hast thou made them all: the earth is full of thy riches" (Psalm 104:24). Much like this awe-inspired acknowledgment of God's creation, Hopkins' poetry often reflects a deep-seated marvel at the natural world, seeing in it the fingerprints of God's creative omnipotence. It might be said that Hopkins did not simply write poetry; he penned doxologies, hymns of praise to God for the gift of beauty manifest in creation.

Hopkins' innovative use of sprung rhythm, a poetic device that he mastered and manipulated with unparalleled skill, served as more than mere poetic form. It was, in essence, his way of mimicking the unpredictable, bursting energy found in nature and, by extension, the dynamic, vivacious presence of God within it. "The world is charged with the grandeur of God," he writes, in a line that encapsulates his theological aesthetic (Hopkins, "God's Grandeur"). Through this, Hopkins suggests that to engage with beauty is to engage with God Himself, an encounter that has the power to move the human heart towards conversion.

In reflecting on the sacramentality of everyday life, Hopkins did not shy away from the complexities and duality of creation. His concept of 'inscape,' the unique essence of every being and thing as an expression of divine creation, invites the observer to look beyond the surface, to perceive the deeper spiritual resonance behind physical appearances. Through this lens, Hopkins proposes that everything in creation bears witness to the divine artist, God, and thus, holds the potential to lead souls to a greater awareness of His presence.

It was in the darkest contrasts of the natural world where Hopkins often found the most profound glimpses of divine beauty. His musings on nature and divinity did not stop at pastoral landscapes or serene visions. Rather, he found a distinct echo of God's voice in the "dearest freshness deep down things" (Hopkins, "God's Grandeur"), a phrase that beautifully articulates his conviction that even in the decay and destruction in nature, there lies a deeper beauty, a spark of divine renewal and hope.

Hopkins' evocation of beauty as a pathway to God did not rest solely on the observation of nature but also in the very act of creating art. He viewed his poetry as a form of prayer, a means of engaging with God through the crafting of language and rhythm. This sacramental view of artistic creation underscores Hopkins' belief in the power of beauty not just to reflect God's grandeur but to act as a vehicle for divine grace, capable of touching and transforming hearts.

Amid a world often clouded by the mundane, Hopkins' works stand as a clarion call to awaken the spiritual senses. "For Christ plays in ten thousand places, Lovely in limbs, and lovely in eyes not his To the Father through the features of men's faces" (Hopkins, "As Kingfishers Catch Fire"). This line encapsulates his vision of Christ's pervasive presence in the world, a presence that beckons the soul to recognize and respond to the divine call hidden in the beauty that surrounds us.

The evangelizing power of Hopkins' poetry lies in its capacity to render the invisible God visible through the tangible reality of beauty. In an age where faith often finds itself challenged by skepticism and secularism, Hopkins' artistic contributions emerge as a vital reminder of the inherently spiritual nature of beauty and its capacity to lead us back to the source of all beauty, God Himself.

In considering the role of art and literature in the service of evangelization, Gerard Manley Hopkins' work illuminates a profound truth: that beauty, in its purest, most authentic form, possesses an innate ability to draw the human heart towards the divine. As such, artists and writers bearing the torch of faith have before them not just an opportunity but a sacred duty to witness to the beauty of God in their creations, thereby participating in the evangelizing mission of the Church.

The intertwining of aesthetics and theology in Hopkins' thought mirrors the incarnational reality of Christianity, where the Word became flesh and dwelt among us. Just as the incarnation reveals the depths of God's love through the tangible reality of Christ's presence, so too does beauty offer a palpable, visceral pathway to encounter God. The vocation of the Christian poet, then, becomes one of echoing the incarnate Word through the beauty of language, a vocation Hopkins embraced with fervor and humility.

In conclusion, Gerard Manley Hopkins' legacy as both a poet and a theological thinker underscores the potency of beauty as a means of evangelization. Through his rich, vivid imagery and profound spiritual insights, he offers a vision of art as an indispensable ally in the quest to draw souls to Christ. Hopkins teaches us that beauty, in all its forms, is not merely an accessory to faith but a vibrant, essential pathway to encountering God. His life and work serve as a beacon, guiding us to witness and respond to the divine beauty that permeates our world, inviting us to a deeper communion with our Creator.

The psalmist's call to "worship the Lord in the beauty of holiness" (Psalm 96:9) finds a resonant echo in Hopkins' poetry, a reminder that in the pursuit of truth and goodness, beauty plays an indispensable role. May we, following in Hopkins' footsteps, remain ever attuned to the divine whisper in the beauty that surrounds us, finding within it a ceaseless source of inspiration, consolation, and evangelizing fervor.

Chapter 9: The Practical Implications of the Illative Sense for Modern Believers

In contemplating the landscape of our contemporary world, one may ponder upon the practical bearings of the illative sense, particularly as discerned through the lens of faith. Living out faith today requires a conscientious engagement with both the seen and unseen, an endeavor that demands a synthesis of reason, imagination, and spirit. For modern believers, the challenge lies not merely in the adherence to doctrinal truths but also in the application of these truths within the complex matrices of daily life. The essence of this challenge is captured succinctly in the words, "Let your light so shine before men, that they may see your good works, and glorify your Father which is in heaven" (Matt. 5:16). The illative sense, as a guide, steers the believer's journey towards embodying faith in actions that resonate with divine truth, thus bearing witness to the transformative power of living a life anchored in God.

The relevance of Newman and Hopkins in today's digital, fractious age cannot be overstated. Their work embodies a profound testament to the enduring nature of faith's journey through the landscapes of literature and theology. For Hopkins, the world itself is charged with the grandeur of God, inviting a perception of the divine in every leaf and stone, which in turn influences how we live our faith amidst the mundane and the miraculous. This perception, deeply rooted in the illative sense, encourages believers to view their environment through a lens of sacramentality, recognizing the inherent goodness and purpose within creation, thus fostering a greater responsibility towards stewardship and environmental consciousness.

In facing the complexities of the contemporary world, believers are called to navigate societal paradigms and cultural narratives with discernment and grace, qualities that the illative sense sharpens through its confluence of reason and faith. Through engaging with literature and art as did Newman and Hopkins, believers can cultivate a more nuanced understanding of God, humanity, and the interplay between them. Such engagement not only enriches the soul but also equips believers with the language and perspective needed to articulate their faith in contexts that may be indifferent or even hostile to religious viewpoints. As the believer's heart and mind expand in understanding, so too does the capacity to live out their faith with authenticity, integrity, and a deeply rooted sense of purpose, bearing witness to the timeless relevance of the illative sense in navigating the human condition and its quest for truth and meaning.

Living Out Faith in the Contemporary World

In an era where secular thought pervades and technology claims dominion over the hours of our lives, the task of living out one's faith appears as both a challenge and a profound opportunity. The contemporary believer finds themselves at the crossroads of historical religious conviction and the rapidly evolving landscape of modern society. It is here, in this liminal space, that the practical implications of the illative sense, as understood by believers, take on new dimensions and urgency.

The illative sense, a nuanced faculty of reasoning towards faith, intertwines the personal, intellectual, and spiritual realms. It beckons the believer to navigate the complexities of the modern world with a heart both discerning and open to the divine whispers in the ordinary. In essence, the illative sense becomes the compass by which believers might chart their course in a world that often seems at odds with the tenets of faith.

For the modern believer, the act of integrating faith into daily life extends beyond the personal to the communal and the global. The scripture reminds us, "Let your light so shine before men, that they may see your good works, and glorify your Father which is in heaven" (Matt. 5:16). Thus, living out faith is not a solitary journey but a vibrant testimony carried out in the marketplace, in the academy, within families, and amongst friends.

Engagement in the arts and literature presents a rich soil for the seeds of faith to germinate and flourish. As the illative sense propels the believer towards a synthesis of knowledge, beauty, and truth, it finds resonance in the literary contributions of believers past. The act of creating, appreciating, and sharing art becomes a sacred dialogue, a means through which the divine is both revealed and encountered.

In the sphere of moral decision-making, the contemporary believer employs the illative sense to navigate the ethical dilemmas of the age. The challenge lies not in the rejection of modernity outright but in discerning how one might faithfully inhabit it. Such discernment requires a deep anchorage in one's faith, coupled with an engagement with the world that is both critical and compassionate.

The illative sense also informs the vocation of the believer, urging them to view their work, whatever it might be, as a form of service to the divine. In this light, professions and daily tasks are imbued with a sacramental quality, transforming routines into rituals, and labor into offerings.

Within the ecclesial community, living out one's faith takes on the dimensions of fellowship and service. The believer, grounded in the love of Christ, is called to mirror that love in acts of generosity, hospitality, and justice. Here, the illative sense cultivates an awareness of the needs of others, inspiring actions that bridge divides and heal wounds.

The contemporary world, with its rapid pace and complex challenges, often breeds isolation and despair. In this context, the believer's witness to hope becomes a beacon of light. Faith, lived out with authenticity and courage, counters the narratives of nihilism with the enduring message of redemption and grace.

Evangelization in the modern age requires creativity and sensitivity to the signs of the times. The illative sense equips believers with the insight to discern these signs, enabling them to communicate the Gospel message in ways that resonate with contemporary hearts and minds.

Educational institutions serve as vital arenas for the integration of faith and reason, fostering environments where the illative sense is nurtured and challenged. Through dialogue and study, believers contribute to a culture that values truth, seeks understanding, and respects the sacred dignity of every person.

In the political realm, living out one's faith demands an engagement that transcends partisanship, embodying principles of justice, peace, and the common good. The illative sense guides the believer in discerning when to lend their voice, when to act, and when to offer a prophetic witness to power.

The care for creation stands as an urgent moral imperative in the contemporary world. The illative sense, rooted in a sacramental view of the world, awakens in the believer a reverence for nature as a reflection of the divine, catalyzing efforts towards environmental stewardship and sustainability.

In navigating the digital landscape, the believer exercises the illative sense by fostering communities of support and platforms for genuine encounter. Amid the noise and distractions, faith lived out in the digital age becomes a testament to the power of human connection and the presence of the divine in virtual spaces.

At the heart of living out one's faith in the contemporary world lies the call to holiness, a journey of becoming that is both deeply personal and intrinsically connected to the lives of others. The illative sense, as a guide in this journey, illumines the path towards a fullness of life in which every thought, word, and deed is an echo of the divine love that sustains the cosmos.

In conclusion, the practical implications of the illative sense for modern believers call for a faith that is both deeply rooted and dynamically engaged with the world. It is a call to bear witness, through the particularities of one's life, to the transformative power of the Gospel. In doing so, believers weave a tapestry of faith that not only enriches their own lives but contributes to the healing and renewal of the world.

The Relevance of Newman and Hopkins Today

In an age characterized by rapid technological advancement and shifting moral landscapes, the theological and literary insights of John Henry Newman and Gerard Manley Hopkins offer a beacon of constancy and depth. These two figures, though operating in different realms of thought and creativity, converge on the understanding that the journey of faith is both a personal and communal quest for truth. Their works, steeped in the richness of Christian tradition and the intricacies of the human experience, speak profoundly to modern believers navigating the complexities of 21st-century life.

Newman's conception of the illative sense, as a faculty of reasoning that moves beyond the purely empirical to embrace the religious dimension of human knowledge, provides a crucial framework for understanding faith in an increasingly secular world. It is a reminder that faith is not contrary to reason but rather a harmonious extension of it, engaging the whole person in a search for meaning that transcends the limits of physical evidence. This approach offers a counter-narrative to the prevailing view that science and faith are inherently at odds, instead advocating for a dialogue between them that enriches rather than diminishes human understanding.

Similarly, Hopkins' unique literary contributions, characterized by their rhythmic beauty and their profound sense of sacramentality, illuminate the presence of the divine in the natural world. His poetry, with its innovative use of sprung rhythm and rich imagery, serves as a call to notice and appreciate the omnipresence of God in creation. In a culture often marked by disconnection from the natural world and one another, Hopkins' work beckons readers back to a sense of wonder and interconnectedness.

The moral and spiritual dilemmas faced by characters in Newman's novels and sermons mirror the ethical challenges confronting individuals today. His narratives, grounded in the complexities of moral decision-making within the context of faith, provide a useful lens through which contemporary believers can examine their own choices and commitments.

The realization that one's actions must be informed by both personal conviction and the teachings of the church resonates with those seeking to live out their faith authentically in a pluralistic society.

In fostering a renaissance of virtue, both Newman and Hopkins establish the arts as a vital means of moral education and spiritual reflection. They exemplify how literature and poetry can cultivate empathy, strengthen moral intuition, and inspire a deeper commitment to the common good. This perspective is especially pertinent in an era where the arts are often undervalued or dismissed as irrelevant to serious moral discourse.

The call to evangelization through beauty, articulated by both thinkers, challenges modern believers to consider how their creative endeavors can witness to the beauty of the Gospel. In a world saturated with images and messages vying for attention, the transformative power of beauty as a path to truth offers a compelling alternative. It invites artists, writers, and all individuals to contribute to a culture that reflects the goodness and creativity of God.

Furthermore, their insights into the nature of sin and redemption speak directly to the heart of the human condition. The recognition of human frailty, coupled with the hope of grace and the promise of redemption, provides guidance and comfort to those navigating personal failings and societal injustices. Their writings encourage a posture of humility, repentance, and open-heartedness toward the transformative power of God's grace.

Both Newman and Hopkins also highlight the importance of the community in the journey of faith. The notion that individuals are not isolated entities but rather part of a larger body of believers has profound implications for how faith is lived out in the contemporary world. It stresses the importance of fellowship, mutual support, and the communal pursuit of truth, all of which are essential in an individualistic and often fragmented society.

The enduring relevance of Newman and Hopkins today can also be seen in their approach to doubt and certainty. Their willingness to engage with doubt, rather than dismiss it outright, offers a path for those wrestling with questions of faith. By acknowledging doubt as an integral part of the journey towards certainty, they provide a model of faith that is dynamic and resilient, capable of withstanding the trials of modern life.

In conclusion, the writings of John Henry Newman and Gerard Manley Hopkins hold significant practical implications for modern believers. Their insights into faith, reason, beauty, and the moral life offer valuable resources for navigating the complexities of contemporary existence. By engaging with their works, individuals today can find guidance, inspiration, and a deeper understanding of what it means to live a life of faith in an ever-changing world. In the intricate dance of light and shadow that characterizes human experience, the perspectives of these two eminent thinkers light the way for all who seek to walk in the path of truth.

As we reflect on the journey ahead, let us recall the words found in the book of Matthew, "Let your light so shine before men, that they may see your good works, and glorify your Father which is in heaven" (Matt. 5:16). In embracing the legacy of Newman and Hopkins, believers today are invited to become beacons of hope and truth, illuminating the path for others in a world thirsty for the light of the Gospel.

Chapter 10: The Critic's Lens: Literary Scholars on Newman and Hopkins

In the realm of literary and theological scholarship, the works of John Henry Newman and Gerard Manley Hopkins have been subjected to a thorough and meticulous examination. Their rich tapestry of writings, infused with a profound sense of faith and a meticulous attention to the linguistic craft, have invited a diverse range of interpretations and critiques. This chapter aims to delve into the academic perspectives that have shone a light on Newman's and Hopkins' unique contributions to both literature and theology. As the psalmist declares, "Thy word is a lamp unto my feet, and a light unto my path" (Ps. 119:105), so too have these scholars sought to illuminate the intricacies of Newman's and Hopkins' paths through the dense forests of faith and doubt.

Newman's approach to literature, often characterized by his intricate prose and philosophical depth, has been regarded by some scholars as a pivotal bridge between the theological and the literary. His use of narrative and metaphor to explore complex theological concepts has not only enriched the literary landscape of his time but has also offered a nuanced method of engaging with faith through the intellect. Similarly, Hopkins' experimental verse and his vivid portrayal of nature's reflection of the divine have captivated literary critics and theologians alike. His sprung rhythm and innovative diction have been viewed as a revolutionary contribution to the poetic form, serving as a vehicle for expressing the ineffable mysteries of God's presence in the world.

However, the critical lens through which scholars view Newman and Hopkins is not without its criticisms. Debates have arisen over the extent to which Newman's theological positions may have constrained his literary imagination, or conversely, elevated it. Questions have also been posed regarding Hopkins' dense imagery and complex syntax, pondering whether his innovative techniques enhance or obscure the spiritual messages he sought to convey. Yet, it is precisely in these debates that the richness of Newman's and Hopkins' works are fully revealed, challenging readers to engage with both the letter and the spirit of their texts.

Amidst these academic discussions, a consensus emerges on one point: both Newman and Hopkins have made indelible marks on the landscape of English literature and Christian theology. Their works serve as beacons, guiding those who tread the delicate line between faith and reason, art and spirituality. As scholars continue to explore the depths of their writings, the dialogue between faith and literature that both Newman and Hopkins so passionately engaged in remains vibrant and profoundly relevant. Their legacy invites a reassessment of not just their own works, but of the very nature of religious expression within the literary canon.

In conclusion, the critical examination of Newman and Hopkins through the lens of literary scholarship has not only heightened our understanding of their individual contributions but has also enriched the broader conversation on the interplay between faith and literature. As we reflect on their literary and theological journey, we are reminded of the enduring power of words to challenge, comfort, and inspire. In the hands of Newman and Hopkins, language becomes a tool for exploring the vast expanse of human experience, guided by the light of faith and the pursuit of truth. Their literary endeavors, measured against the backdrop of academic critique, stand as a testament to the abiding significance of seeking God within the tapestry of creation.

Academic Perspectives on Newman's Literary Contributions

Within the realm of literary scholarship, the oeuvre of John Henry Newman stands as a monumental edifice, bridging the chasms between theology, philosophy, and literature with unparalleled finesse. Scholars, over the years, have delved deep into the rich tapestry of Newman's writings, unearthing the nuanced layers that comprise his literary contributions. This chapter endeavors to shed light on the academic discourses surrounding Newman's literature, particularly focusing on its theological underpinnings and moral implications, which resonate with the profound biblical injunction to "Let your light so shine before men, that they may see your good works, and glorify your Father which is in heaven" (Matt. 5:16).

At the heart of Newman's literary corpus lies the profound synthesis of intellectual rigor and spiritual fervor. Scholars argue that Newman's unique literary voice is not merely a vehicle for aesthetic expression but a means of theological exploration and moral instruction. His works, imbued with a sense of divine purpose, echo the Pauline exhortation to "prove all things; hold fast that which is good" (1 Thess. 5:21), inviting readers to embark on a journey of intellectual and spiritual discovery.

The narrative elegance of Newman's sermons, for instance, is renowned for its capacity to capture the complexities of faith with both clarity and depth. Literary critics have highlighted how these sermons transcend the conventional homiletic boundaries, weaving together theological insight and human experience in a manner that is both intellectually stimulating and spiritually uplifting. This blending of the human and divine in Newman's narratives underscores the incarnational reality that "the Word was made flesh, and dwelt among us" (John 1:14), highlighting the immanence of the divine in the minutiae of human existence.

Newman's novel, "Loss and Gain", also garners significant attention from scholars for its exploration of the tumultuous journey of faith. This narrative, set against the backdrop of the Oxford Movement, provides a rich literary canvas painting the intricate interplay between doubt and faith, reason and revelation. Academic critics assert that through this narrative, Newman elucidates the convoluted path toward spiritual certainty, echoing the biblical affirmation that "faith is the substance of things hoped for, the evidence of things not seen" (Heb. 11:1).

Further, Newman's extensive correspondences offer a fascinating insight into the mind of a man grappling with the profoundest questions of his time. Literary scholars have extensively analyzed these letters, unearthing the intellectual ferment and the personal crises that fueled Newman's theological and literary output. These epistles serve as a testament to Newman's relentless quest for truth, undergirded by the biblical principle that "ye shall know the truth, and the truth shall make you free" (John 8:32).

Moreover, Newman's "Apologia Pro Vita Sua" stands as a monumental work within his literary portfolio, providing not only a defense of his spiritual journey but also a compelling narrative of personal transformation. Scholars often cite this work as a masterclass in autobiographical writing, where Newman employs his literary acumen to navigate the treacherous waters of religious controversy and personal strife. It is a literary embodiment of the Psalmist's declaration, "He brought me up also out of an horrible pit, out of the miry clay, and set my feet upon a rock, and established my goings" (Psalm 40:2).

Academic discourse on Newman's poetry also merits attention, with critics highlighting the theological richness and literary sophistication of his verse. His poems, such as "The Dream of Gerontius", capture the existential angst and the hope of redemption, encapsulated in the Christian narrative of death and resurrection. Scholars draw parallels between Newman's poetic visions and the biblical imagery of redemption and eternal life, demonstrating how Newman's literary craft serves as a conduit for theological reflection.

The critical acclaim for Newman's literary contributions, however, is not without its detractors. Some scholars critique Newman's works for their perceived doctrinal rigidity and ideological underpinning, arguing that his literature often privileges theological orthodoxy over artistic expression. Yet, even in these critiques, the depth of Newman's commitment to his faith and the intellectual vigor of his literary pursuits is evident, reflecting a life lived in accordance with the dictate to "work out your own salvation with fear and trembling" (Philippians 2:12).

In examining Newman's literary contributions, scholars also explore the dialogical nature of his writings, especially his engagement with contemporaneous theological and philosophical debates. This aspect of Newman's work demonstrates his belief in the power of literature to catalyze intellectual discourse and spiritual reflection, embodying the contention that "Iron sharpeneth iron; so a man sharpeneth the countenance of his friend" (Proverbs 27:17).

Furthermore, the educational philosophies espoused by Newman, particularly within "The Idea of a University", have garnered considerable academic interest. His vision for an educational system that integrates the cultivation of the intellect with moral and spiritual development is hailed as revolutionary, providing a literary blueprint for a holistic approach to education that mirrors the biblical exhortation to "Train up a child in the way he should go: and when he is old, he will not depart from it" (Proverbs 22:6).

In synthesis, the academic perspectives on Newman's literary contributions reveal a complex tapestry of theological inquiry, philosophical introspection, and literary innovation. His works, deeply rooted in the Christian tradition, continue to inspire and challenge readers, scholars, and believers, reminding us of the power of literature as a medium for exploring the mysteries of faith, the realities of human existence, and the path to divine truth.

As the discourse on Newman's literary and theological legacy unfolds, it becomes increasingly clear that his writings not only offer a window into the soul of a man deeply committed to his faith but also serve as a beacon for those navigating the tumultuous seas of doubt and belief. The enduring relevance of Newman's literary contributions lies in their capacity to engage the intellect, stir the heart, and inspire the soul, fulfilling the scriptural call to "study to shew thyself approved unto God, a workman that needeth not to be ashamed, rightly dividing the word of truth" (2 Timothy 2:15).

In the final analysis, the academic exploration of John Henry Newman's literary corpus underscores not only his indelible impact on the landscape of English literature and theology but also illuminates the broader discourse on the intersecting pathways of faith, reason, and art. It is a testament to the enduring power of literature to transcend temporal and spatial boundaries, fostering a dialogue that transcends generations, cultures, and creeds—a dialogue that, at its best, can lead us closer to the ineffable truths that lie at the heart of human and divine communion.

Hopkins' Place in Modern Theological Discussion

In the tapestry of modern theological discussion, the thread representing Gerard Manley Hopkins, S.J., showcases a vibrant hue that is both subtle and arresting. Hopkins, unlike His contemporaries, delved deep into the heart of what it means to perceive God's grandeur in the mundane. His work, deeply embedded in the richness of God's creation, offers a fresh lens through which one might view the divine interaction with the world. "The world is charged with the grandeur of God," he writes, inviting us to see the sacred in the profane, the extraordinary in the ordinary (Hopkins, "God's Grandeur").

His place in modern theological discourse is distinguished by his unique approach to nature and the divine. Hopkins does not merely observe nature; he sees it as a manifestation of God's ongoing creation, a reflection of His beauty and grace. In an era where faith often grapples with the disenchantment of the world, Hopkins' poetry serves as a reminder of the omni-presence of the divine. "Christ plays in ten thousand places, lovely in limbs, and lovely in eyes not his," he marvels, emphasizing the ubiquity of Christ in the world and in mankind (Hopkins, "As Kingfishers Catch Fire").

Theologically, Hopkins' writings underscore the importance of individual experience of God. This emphasis on personal encounter with the divine echoes the theological movements of the 20th and 21st centuries, which seek to understand faith as a lived experience. Hopkins' poetry, with its rich imagery and innovative use of sprung rhythm, embodies this personal and immersive approach to experiencing God.

In academic circles, Hopkins has been subject to a myriad of interpretations, each seeking to unravel the theological and philosophical underpinnings of his work. Some scholars highlight his contributions to sacramental theology, noting how his descriptions of nature often carry sacramental overtones, suggesting that the material world is a conduit of God's grace. "There lives the dearest freshness deep down things,"

Hopkins writes, pointing to the intrinsic goodness and sanctity of creation which reflects God's grace and beauty (Hopkins, "God's Grandeur").

Others focus on Hopkins' exploration of human identity and its relationship with the divine. His poem "As kingfishers catch fire, dragonflies draw flame" suggests a divine spark within each creature, a unique expression of God's creative will. This aligns with modern discussions on dignity and sanctity of life, showcasing Hopkins' relevance in contemporary debates surrounding identity and spirituality.

In discussions of suffering and despair, Hopkins' "terrible sonnets" present a poignant exploration of the dark night of the soul, reflecting modern theology's engagement with theodicy and the problem of evil. His raw honesty and deep anguish resonate with those who struggle, offering a theological lens through which to view suffering—not as absence of God but as a profound, albeit painful, encounter with the divine.

Ecological theology, too, finds a friend in Hopkins, whose work presages contemporary concerns about environmental degradation and the sacramentality of the earth. Hopkins' vision of a world imbued with God's presence compels a closer look at our ecological crisis through a theological and ethical lens, challenging us to stewardship and reverence for creation.

Within the context of evangelization, Hopkins champions the use of beauty as a means to draw souls to God. His poetry, rich in aesthetic quality and spiritual depth, exemplifies how art and literature can be powerful tools in the New Evangelization, speaking to the hearts of those who yearn for beauty and truth.

The discussions of sin, redemption, and grace in Hopkins' work further cement his place in contemporary theology. His insistence on the redemptive potential of grace, even in the bleakest of circumstances, offers a counter-narrative to despair, emphasizing hope and transformation in Christ.

Finally, Hopkins' place in modern theological discourse is marked by his profound influence on the dialogue between faith and science. His keen observation of natural phenomena, combined with a deep spiritual insight, presents a model for engaging with the natural sciences in a way that enriches rather than contradicts faith.

The interdisciplinary nature of Hopkins' work, straddling the worlds of poetry, theology, philosophy, and science, makes his contribution to modern theological discussion both unique and invaluable. It is through his eyes that many have come to see the world anew, infused with the grandeur of God.

As modern theology continues to wrestle with questions of faith, meaning, and the place of humanity in the cosmos, Hopkins' voice remains relevant, offering insights that are at once timeless and timely. His work challenges us to look beyond the surface, to find the divine whisper in the wind, the footprints of Christ in the sand. "For Christ plays in ten thousand places," indeed, and it is through Hopkins' eyes that many have learned to see this divine play more clearly (Hopkins, "As Kingfishers Catch Fire").

In sum, Gerard Manley Hopkins occupies a crucial place in the landscape of modern theological discussion, bridging the gap between the sacred and the secular, the divine and the mundane. His contributions continue to inspire, challenge, and enlighten those who seek to understand the mystery of faith in a rapidly changing world. As scholars and theologians delve into the depths of Hopkins' work, they discover a wellspring of wisdom that speaks to the core of human experience, offering a beacon of hope and beauty in a world in desperate need of both.

Chapter 11: A Synthesis of Illative Imagination and Faith

At the heart of the dialogue between John Henry Newman and Gerard Manley Hopkins lies a profound synthesis of illative imagination and faith, a confluence where the tributaries of literary talent and divine belief merge into a vigorous stream of Christian witness. This chapter aims to elucidate that synthesis, charting its implications for both the individual soul and the communal body of the Church. The union of an imaginative approach to theology with a deeply rooted faith is not merely a theoretical nicety; rather, it is a dynamic process through which the ineffable is rendered accessible, whereby the divine spark within humanity can be kindled into a flame.

The foundation of this synthesis is an understanding that imagination, when allied with faith, becomes an instrument of divine truth. It is not enough to assert, as scripture does in *Hebrews 11:1*, that "faith is the substance of things hoped for, the evidence of things not seen". One must also recognize the role of the imagination in giving shape to this hope, in manifesting the evidence of the unseen in the heart and mind of the believer. Through literary creation, Newman and Hopkins practiced and advocated for a type of imaginative envisioning that pushes beyond the boundaries of empirical reality, inviting engagement with spiritual truths through metaphor, rhythm, and symbol.

This is not to say that their approach dismisses reason or empirical enquiry. Indeed, Newman's discussion of the illative sense underscores the integration of reason and faith, suggesting that a nuanced understanding of truth encompasses more than logical deduction. It is within this broader understanding that imagination finds its rightful place, enabling the believer to perceive and grasp the multifaceted dimensions of divine reality that bare reason alone might miss. For Hopkins, the natural world was imbued with the grandeur of God, an endless source of inspiration and revelation, demanding a poetic response that could articulate the inarticulate, that could sing what the eye beholds in silence.

However, this synthesis of illative imagination and faith requires a cultivation of both virtues. As with any endeavor worthy of pursuit, it demands discipline, practice, and a community of support. Literature and the arts serve not only as expressions of individual insight but as communal resources for spiritual growth and moral reflection. They embody the ongoing dialogue between the human and the divine, a dialogue that shapes and is shaped by the illative imagination. As believers engage with literary works inspired by faith, they are invited into a deeper relationship with the divine, encouraged to explore the recesses of their own belief and inspired to express their understanding through their unique talents.

In conclusion, the synthesis of illative imagination and faith as demonstrated through the works and lives of Newman and Hopkins offers a compelling vision for the integration of spirituality and artistic endeavor. It challenges believers to consider how their faith informs their creative output and vice versa, how their imaginative efforts can deepen and broaden their understanding of God. In a world often fragmented by dichotomies between faith and reason, between the spiritual and the material, the legacy of Newman and Hopkins stands as a testament to the power and potential of their union. Thus, the believers are called not only to behold the beauty of the Lord but also to reflect it in their lives and works, as is exhorted in *Psalm 27:4*, that one thing have they desired of the Lord, that will they seek after; that they may dwell in the house of the Lord all the days of their life, to behold the beauty of the Lord, and to inquire in his temple.

The Unified Theory of Newman and Hopkins

Within the intellectual and spiritual landscapes fashioned by John Henry Newman and Gerard Manley Hopkins, one discerns a remarkable confluence of thought, particularly concerning the illative sense - a term Newman famously elaborated upon, and Hopkins, though not explicitly, lived out through his poetry. This synthesis, a melding of illative imagination and faith, offers a profound insight into how literature can serve as a vessel for divine truth, leading the soul towards God.

Newman's exploration of the illative sense, primarily in his philosophical works, articulated the process by which an individual arrives at certainty in matters of faith. This process, far from being a simple deduction of reason, incorporates the whole being, engaging the intellect, imagination, and emotional faculties. It's in this nuanced understanding of belief that Newman's thoughts harmonize with Hopkins' poetic practice, where the latter's works serve as a testament to experiencing God through the beauty and particularities of creation.

In pondering the divine, both thinkers exhibit a staunch resistance to the reduction of faith to mere intellectual assent. For Newman, faith is deeply personal, requiring an active participation of the will; "Let your light so shine before men, that they may see your good works, and glorify your Father which is in heaven" (Matt. 5:16). Hopkins' poetry echoes this sentiment, as he invites readers to see God's grandeur in the world around them, thus moving from observation to contemplation, and, ideally, to love.

The synthesis of imagination and faith thus forms the crux of their unified theory. Imagination, as employed by both, isn't a mere fancy but a crucial cognitive faculty that bridges the gap between the known and the unknown, between the seen and the unseen. In Hopkins' verse, one finds the natural world imbued with an intensity of being, or 'inscape', that reveals the Creator's presence. This palpable sense of God's immanence serves to awaken the spiritual senses, guiding the soul towards a deeper, more intimate communion with Him.

Moreover, Newman's insistence on the personal nature of faith - a journey that involves doubt, struggle, and eventual assent - mirrors Hopkins' own spiritual odyssey, as documented in his diaries and letters. Both men experienced periods of profound spiritual desolation, yet it was through these trials that their faith matured, solidified, and became all the more convincing to them and, through their works, to others.

This journey of faith, marked by an illative process that engages the whole person, necessarily entails a moral transformation. Here again, Newman and Hopkins converge in their understanding that true faith bears fruit in virtuous living. As Newman posits, the assent of faith is not merely intellectual but moral, requiring one to live in accordance with God's laws. Hopkins' poetry, with its frequent meditations on beauty, nature, and grace, serves as a vivid reminder of the goodness of God's creation and our duty to steward it responsibly.

The evangelizing power of literature, a theme close to both thinkers, further illustrates the practical implications of their unified theory. Newman's sermons, essays, and novels, together with Hopkins' poetry, exemplify how art and literature can mediate the Christian faith, making the truths of religion accessible and compelling to the modern mind. For Newman, literature acts as a means to evangelize, to reach those outside the fold; for Hopkins, it serves to reveal God's presence in the world, to awaken a sense of awe and wonder that leads back to the Creator.

In their respective endeavors, both Newman and Hopkins demonstrate a profound understanding of the role of beauty in the religious experience. Beauty, for them, is not merely aesthetic but a vehicle of divine grace that draws the soul closer to God. This appreciation for beauty as a conduit of spiritual truth challenges the sometimes utilitarian approach to faith seen in the modern world, advocating instead for a recognition of the transcendent aspects of religion.

The unified theory of Newman and Hopkins, with its emphasis on the integration of imagination, faith, and morality, thus offers a robust framework for understanding the complex dynamics of religious belief. It acknowledges the limitations of human reason while celebrating the capacity of literature and art to convey spiritual truths in ways that reason alone cannot.

In conclusion, this synthesis of illative imagination and faith fashioned by Newman and Hopkins presents a compelling argument for the indispensability of literature and the arts in the life of faith. Through their collective works, they illustrate how the imaginative faculty, when sanctified and directed towards God, becomes an indispensable tool for spiritual insight, moral edification, and ultimately, for evangelization. Hence, their unified theory remains a beacon for those navigating the waters of faith and doubt, seeking to reconcile the heart's affections with the mind's assertions in the pursuit of Divine Truth.

As we continue to delve into the rich theological and literary legacies of Newman and Hopkins, it becomes increasingly evident that their contributions transcend their historical moment. In a world hungering for meaning, their unified theory shines as a testament to the power of faith informed by reason, beauty, and a profound sense of God's immanence in the world. It is a theory that calls not just for contemplation but for engagement - an invitation to experience the divine through the beauty of creation, the rigor of thought, and the purity of living.

In this light, the synthesis offered by Newman and Hopkins does not merely represent a theoretical intersection of ideas but a lived experience of faith. It challenges contemporary believers to look beyond the superficial, to engage with the world, with literature, and with one another in a manner that is deeply informed by faith, hope, and love. Thus, the legacy of these two thinkers provides not only a rich source of theological and literary insight but also a model for how to live out one's faith in a complex and often confusing world.

Their unified theory, then, stands as a call to action - a reminder of the power of beauty, the validity of imagination in matters of faith, and the importance of living out one's beliefs with integrity and compassion. As we reflect on their contributions, let us be inspired to employ our own gifts in service to God and one another, ever mindful of the enduring truth that beauty, in all its forms, serves as a pathway to the divine, guiding us ever closer to the heart of God.

Literary Paths to Discovering God

In the realm of faith, where the tangible meets the transcendent, literature emerges as a bridge over which the seeker may cross into the divine embrace. This journey, illuminated by the luminous minds of figures such as Newman and Hopkins, unveils the illative sense as not merely an intellectual exercise but a deep, resonant call from the heart of God. It is through the tapestry of narrative, poetry, and prose that the soul begins its pilgrimage towards understanding and ultimately, belief.

As the scriptures say, "Faith cometh by hearing, and hearing by the word of God" (Rom. 10:17). This divine hearing, we propose, extends beyond the spoken or preached word, encompassing also the literary expressions that echo the multifaceted voice of God. Through the works of devout authors and poets, the whisper of the Holy Spirit can be discerned, leading the receptive heart to a fuller realization of divine truth.

Literature, in its essence, is a mirror reflecting the complexities and simplicities of the human condition. As Newman keenly observed, it is in these reflections that God's presence can be most acutely perceived. For in every man's story, in every flight of the imagination, lies the potential to uncover a facet of the divine mystery. Literature thus becomes a sanctified ground, a place where faith is both explored and affirmed.

Hopkins' poetry, infused with an intense spiritual ardor and a remarkable sensitivity to nature's beauty, exemplifies this sanctification of the written word. His famed sprung rhythm and innovative diction capture not just the eye of the reader but the soul, urging it to see God's grandeur in all things. Hopkins' artistic endeavor was not mere poetic experimentation; rather, it was an act of faith, a testament to his unshakable belief in a God who is both immanent and transcendent.

This synthesis of faith and literature is not a mere juxtaposition but a deep integration of the two, a realization that the quest for God does not proceed on abstract theological discourse alone but also through the concrete, life-affirming medium of art. Literature, with its capacity to convey human emotions, to tell stories that strike at the heart of our existence, offers a unique pathway to the divine, a path paved with beauty and truth.

Indeed, the spiritual dimension of literature cannot be overlooked. Throughout history, the lives of the saints and the diligent pursuit of holiness have been captured in texts that continue to inspire and edify. These writings, though varied in form and style, share a common purpose: to draw the reader closer to the heart of God. They serve as reminders that the journey of faith is both personal and universal, a voyage that each must undertake, yet one that connects us to the vast communion of believers.

The proliferation of religious themes in literature points to the inherent need of humanity to grapple with the divine. This need transcends cultural, historical, and linguistic barriers, manifesting in works as diverse as the Confessions of Augustine to the contemporary novels that explore themes of redemption, sacrifice, and the search for meaning. Each work contributes to the ongoing dialogue between God and man, a conversation that is both ancient and ever-new.

Through the prism of Newman's and Hopkins' literary contributions, we see the potential of the written word not just to inform but to transform. Their work exemplifies how literature can be an instrument of God's grace, touching hearts and changing lives. It stands as a testament to the power of the literary imagination to illuminate the path to God, guiding the faithful and the seeker alike towards a deeper, more profound understanding of the divine.

Moreover, the exploration of the literary paths to discovering God serves not only as a reflection on the past but also as a beacon for the future. In an age where faith is often sidelined, the marriage of literature and spirituality offers a compelling response, a way to rekindle the flame of belief in the hearts of men and women inundated by the secular. It demonstrates that the search for God is as relevant today as it was in the time of Newman and Hopkins.

It is our hope that this exploration awakens a renewed appreciation for the role of literature in the spiritual journey. Let the words of the poets and the stories of the saints remind us that God speaks not only from the pulpit or the altar but also from the pages of a book. The call to faith, resounding through the ages in myriad forms, invites us to open our hearts to the illative imagination, to see beyond the written word to the Word made flesh.

This literary path to discovering God is, in essence, a call to contemplation, a challenge to see the world and our place in it with eyes wide open to the divine. It beckons us to delve deeper into the mystery of existence, guided by the light of faith and the beauty of the written word. In doing so, we not only enrich our understanding but also fortify our hearts for the journey ahead.

As we traverse this path, let us remember the words "Let your light so shine before men, that they may see your good works, and glorify your Father which is in heaven" (Matt. 5:16). Literature, in its highest form, serves this very purpose: to shine a light on the truth, to glorify God through the beauty of creation, and to lead souls to the eternal embrace of the Father.

In conclusion, the literary paths to discovering God are as varied as they are profound. Through the works of Newman and Hopkins, as well as countless others who have used their talents to explore and express their faith, we are given a map—a map that leads us through the human experience to the heart of divine reality. It is a journey worth undertaking, a quest that enriches the mind, awakens the soul, and brings us ever closer to the God who seeks us in return.

Chapter 12: Future Paths: The Illative Sense in the 21st Century

As we stand at the precipice of a new era, the value of the illative sense as articulated by both Newman and Hopkins presents an enduring beacon for navigating the complexities of faith in the 21st century. This chapter endeavours to chart the course of this navigational tool, exploring its potential to guide contemporary literature and theology through the ever-evolving landscape of belief and understanding.

At the heart of the discussion is the immutable truth that literature, with its rich tapestry of narrative and metaphor, continues to offer a fertile ground for the exploration and expression of faith. The illative sense, that instinctual leap towards belief and understanding, remains as pertinent today as it was in the times of Newman and Hopkins. It is in the power of language and story that we find paths to articulate the ineffable, to make sense of the divine in the minutiae of human experience.

The works of Newman and Hopkins stood as testaments to the potency of literary endeavor in bridging the gap between the human and the divine. As we venture further into the 21st century, it becomes increasingly apparent that literature's role in the formulation of faith and moral understanding can't be underestimated. The stories we tell, the poems we write, the narratives we construct - all serve as conduits for the illative sense, guiding us towards deeper truths and more profound understandings of our place in the cosmos.

Moreover, the burgeoning dialogue between science and religion offers new vistas for the illative sense to manifest. Here, literature and theology can play a pivotal role in framing these discussions, offering narratives that reconcile empirical discovery with spiritual insight. "For the invisible things of him from the creation of the world are clearly seen, being understood by the things that are made, even his eternal power and

Godhead" (Rom. 1:20). The illative sense, then, becomes an interpretive key, unlocking the mysteries that lie at the confluence of faith and reason.

Yet, the challenges of post-modernity, with its suspicion of grand narratives and objective truths, demand a recontextualization of the illative sense. The path forward is one of dialogue and engagement, where the voices of Newman and Hopkins can offer wisdom and insight. The task is not to retreat into the comfortable bastions of tradition but to venture forth into the arena of contemporary discourse, armed with the transformative power of literature and theology.

This is not to say that the journey will be without its trials. The landscape of the 21st century is one of plurality and diversity, where competing voices vie for attention and influence. Yet, it is precisely in this milieu that the illative sense can serve as a guiding principle, helping to navigate the complexities of modern belief and skepticism. As the Apostle Paul reminds us, "Now faith is the substance of things hoped for, the evidence of things not seen" (Heb. 11:1). It is through the cultivation of an illative sense, honed by literature and theology, that faith can find its footing in an uncertain world.

The call, then, is for writers, theologians, and believers to engage with the spirit of the age, to harness the illative sense as a tool for understanding and communication. In doing so, we can embark on a journey that not only honours the legacy of Newman and Hopkins but also charts a course towards a future where faith and reason coalesce in the creation of a more just and compassionate world.

The path forward is one of integration and synthesis, where the insights of the past are melded with the realities of the present to forge a way into the future. It is a journey that demands courage, imagination, and an unwavering commitment to the quest for truth. As we traverse this landscape, the illative sense becomes not just a guide, but a companion, lighting the way towards a horizon brimming with possibility and hope.

In conclusion, the illative sense, as explored through the works of Newman and Hopkins, offers a potent tool for engaging with the realities of the 21st century. It is through literature and theology that we can navigate the complexities of faith and understanding, drawing closer to the divine even as we grapple with the questions and challenges of our time. Let us then embrace this journey with open hearts and minds, ever mindful of the promise that lies in the pursuit of truth and the power of the illative sense to illuminate our path.

The Continued Relevance of Newman and Hopkins

In the ongoing journey through the corridors of time, the works and thoughts of John Henry Newman and Gerard Manley Hopkins remain not mere footprints of the past but beacons of the present, guiding the modern soul in its pursuit of the Divine. It is within the intricate weave of their literary and theological endeavors that contemporary seekers find a roadmap to navigate the complexities of faith and reason. The 21st century, with its rapid technological advances and shifting societal values, demands a reassessment of their contributions, particularly in the realm of the illative sense, as it pertains to understanding and experiencing God in a profoundly personal and intellectual manner.

It is prime to acknowledge that the illative sense, as expounded by Newman, serves as a pivotal bridge between the realms of subjective intuition and objective truth. This union finds a harmonious echo in Hopkins' poetry, where the marvels of God's creation and the nuanced experiences of faith are captured with an almost transcendent clarity. As the world becomes increasingly secularized, the significance of their approaches to faith—rooted in the profound and the beautiful—cannot be overstated.

Indeed, Newman's perspective that faith is both a gift and a choice, an act that involves the deepest faculties of man—intellect, will, and heart— speaks directly to the contemporary condition. The recognition that belief is not merely a passive state but an active engagement with truth resonates with modern hearts seeking authenticity and depth in their spiritual journey.

Similarly, Hopkins' insistence on finding God in the grandeur and minutiae of the natural world offers a counter-narrative to the prevailing sense of disconnection and alienation encountered by many today. His poetic insistence on the presence of Christ in every aspect of creation ("Christ plays in ten thousand places, lovely in limbs, and lovely in eyes not his") provides a spiritual and aesthetic framework that is deeply relevant for a generation grappling with ecological crisis and seeking a reconnection with the natural world.

The integration of faith and intellect as demonstrated by both Newman and Hopkins proposes a model of Christian intellectualism that is sorely needed in today's academic and cultural climates. In an age where faith is often sidelined in intellectual discourse, their works remind us that true understanding encompasses both the seen and the unseen, the empirical and the spiritual.

Moreover, their conviction that art and literature are not mere embellishments of life but essential pathways to the Divine offers a powerful antidote to the utilitarian and often reductive perspectives dominant in contemporary society. The beauty inherent in Hopkins' verse and the depth of Newman's prose invite modern minds to transcend the mundane, to see beyond the material, and to appreciate the sacramental vision of reality.

In an era marked by individualism and fragmentation, the communal aspect of faith—emphasized by both thinkers—also bears relevance. Newman's idea of the Church as a living continuity of faith and Hopkins' lived experience of faith within the Jesuit community both highlight the importance of communal witness and the transmission of belief through shared traditions and liturgies.

The challenge of evangelization, a theme both Newman and Hopkins addressed in their own ways, takes on new dimensions in the digital age. Newman's advocacy for a reasoned, literate apologetics and Hopkins' example of evangelization through beauty provide models for contemporary believers seeking to share their faith in an increasingly disenchanted world.

Furthermore, the concept of the illative sense itself offers valuable insight for a culture overwhelmed by information yet starving for wisdom. Newman's emphasis on the holistic integration of knowledge, where truth is discerned through the convergence of evidence, experience, and intuition, provides a much-needed methodology for navigating the complexities of modern life and belief.

The moral landscape, too, finds guidance in their works. Newman's discussions on conscience and Hopkins' portrayal of sin and grace reflect the perennial human struggle with right and wrong, offering insights into the nature of ethical living in a morally ambiguous world. Their conviction that morality cannot be divorced from spirituality continues to challenge a society often tempted to compartmentalize ethics from belief.

In the sphere of education, where the purpose and means of learning are hotly debated, the educational philosophies of Newman and Hopkins, with their emphasis on the formation of the whole person and the pursuit of truth, offer a corrective to the increasingly specialized and secularized approaches prevalent in contemporary academe.

It is in the power of language, too, that their continued relevance is felt. Newman's mastery of rhetoric and Hopkins' innovative poetics both attest to the transformative power of words—imbued with the capacity to illuminate truth, evoke beauty, and awaken faith. Their works stand as testament to the potential of literature not only to reflect but to shape the human experience of the Divine.

Finally, in the personal realm of suffering, doubt, and search for meaning —themes ever-present in the lives and writings of Newman and Hopkins —modern readers find companions for their own spiritual odysseys. Their honest grappling with the mysteries of faith, expressed with both intellectual rigor and poetic sensitivity, offers solace and encouragement to those navigating the dark nights of the soul in an often indifferent world.

In conclusion, the continued relevance of Newman and Hopkins in the 21st century is undiminished. Their contributions to theology, literature, and the understanding of faith in the modern world remain vital, offering rich resources for intellectual and spiritual renewal. As we navigate the challenges and opportunities of this era, their voices—profound, eloquent, and deeply human—invite us to a deeper engagement with the mysteries of faith, the beauty of creation, and the pursuit of Truth itself.

The Illative Sense in Contemporary Literature and Theology

As we navigate the roadmap outlined by the thoughts and insights of Newman and Hopkins, it becomes apparent that their journey has not ended. Rather, it has merely paved the way for contemporary discourse to explore the intertwined relationship between literature, theology, and the illative sense in our modern context. This chapter embarks on scrutinizing how the illative sense, as conceptualized by Newman and manifested in the work of Hopkins, finds its echo in the literary and theological works of the 21st century.

The illative sense, articulated as the capacity to discern and assent to truth within the realm of complex ideas, has not lost its potency. In an age where information overwhelms and skepticism prevails, the gentle guide of intuition and insight remains a beacon of wisdom. Literary figures and theologians alike wield this sense to navigate through narratives and scriptural interpretations, drawing out meanings that transcend the immediate and the obvious.

In contemporary literature, the illative sense manifests through narratives that wrestle with existential questions and divine mysteries. Just as the Psalmist declares, "Thy word is a lamp unto my feet, and a light unto my path" (Psalm 119:105), modern literary works continue to shine a light on the path toward understanding and faith. These narratives embody a journey of the soul, wherein characters and readers alike are invited to explore depths of meaning, morality, and belief. It is in this exploration that the illative sense operates, guiding through intuition, towards a deeper truth.

Theological discourse, too, has found a renewed interest in the illative sense. Just as Newman proposed, the journey toward faith is often a personal and intuitive one, threading through reason but not bound by it alone. Contemporary theologians draw upon this insight, proposing that faith's ascent requires more than empirical evidence; it calls for a leap guided by the heart's illumination. This approach honors the complexity of divine mystery, advocating for a faith that embraces doubt and certainty alike.

Despite the shifts in societal norms and technological advances, the core human thirst for meaning and connection with the divine remains unchanged. The illative sense, therefore, serves as a critical tool in contemporary literature and theology, enabling an engagement with faith that is both intellectually robust and deeply personal. It offers a framework within which contemporary issues and ancient truths can converse, shedding light on the path toward understanding and belief.

The influence of Newman and Hopkins endures, not as relics of the past, but as living inspirations for the present. Their insights into the illative sense and its role in faith formation continue to resonate, providing a lens through which to view contemporary challenges. In literature, this sense enlivens narratives with layers of meaning, while in theology, it invites a nuanced approach to understanding divine revelation.

Furthermore, the integration of the illative sense in modern educational frameworks reveals its versatility and relevance. Literature and theology courses encourage students to engage with texts and doctrines not merely as observers but as participants in a dialogue guided by intuition and critical thinking. This pedagogical approach cultivates a generation capable of navigating complexities with an anchored faith.

The synergy between literature and theology, facilitated by the illative sense, fosters a multidimensional exploration of faith. This exploration transcends doctrinal divides, inviting a communal journey toward understanding. It is in this shared journey that the potential for genuine dialogue and unity emerges, speaking to the core of Newman and Hopkins' legacy.

As we look to the future, the enduring relevance of the illative sense suggests paths yet to be tread. In an era marked by rapid change and uncertainty, the need for a compass that navigates through intuition, reason, and faith becomes all the more pressing. Literature and theology, enriched by this sense, offer beacons of hope and understanding in the quest for truth.

Contemplating the vast landscape of contemporary literature and theology, one can discern the ripples created by Newman and Hopkins. Their insights into the illative sense continue to inspire, challenging authors and theologians to embark on creative and thoughtful explorations of faith. Through their legacy, the dialogue between the divine and the human endures, evolving yet anchored in the timeless quest for understanding and belief.

The challenge for contemporary thinkers lies not in abandoning the foundations laid by Newman and Hopkins but in building upon them. In an age defined by pluralism and interconnectivity, the illative sense offers a means to navigate the diverse expressions of faith and human experience. It invites an openness to the transcendent, grounded in a discerning engagement with the world.

As literary works and theological discourse continue to probe the depths of the human condition, the illative sense serves as a critical ally. It enables a journey that embraces complexity, celebrates mystery, and culminates in a faith that is both reasoned and deeply felt. This journey, illuminated by the insights of Newman and Hopkins, remains a vibrant testament to the power of literature and theology to guide, inspire, and transform.

In conclusion, the illative sense, as expounded by Newman and exemplified by Hopkins, finds a dynamic expression in contemporary literature and theology. It remains a vital tool for discerning truth amidst the complexities of the 21st century, offering a pathway to faith that is intellectually and spiritually enriching. As we venture forth, the legacy of Newman and Hopkins serves as a beacon, guiding the way toward a deeper understanding and a more profound faith.

Therefore, let us embrace the journey ahead with the illative sense as our compass, inspired by the legacy of Newman and Hopkins. Let the light of literature and theology guide us through the uncertainties of our times, leading us toward a faith that is as reasoned as it is heartfelt, as personal as it is universal. For in this journey lies the promise of discovery, the potential for dialogue, and the hope of unity in our quest for the divine.

The Last Quill Stroke

In embarking upon the final leg of our exploration, we come to an intimate juncture—the closure that is not an ending, but a commencement. The journey through the mindscapes of John Henry Newman and Gerard Manley Hopkins has led us to a precipice, overlooking a vista where faith and literature intertwine so profoundly as to become indistinguishable. Like a quill poised over parchment, our exploration hovers, ready to draw conclusions yet reluctant to cease the flow of ink.

The essence of Newman and Hopkins' contributions lies not merely in their theological or literary outputs, but in the nuanced interplay between belief and expression, between the divine and the human word. As we have traversed the realms in which they operated, a common theme emerged— a theme deeply entrenched in the fabric of Christian thought and articulated explicitly within biblical narratives. "In the beginning was the Word, and the Word was with God, and the Word was God" (John 1:1). This foundational premise underpins the endeavors of both men, casting light on their literary and spiritual quests.

Newman's illative sense, intricate in its construct, advocates for a personal assent to faith that is immersive and experiential. Literature, within his framework, becomes a conduit through which the divine can communicate, touching souls in a manner that doctrinal discourse alone cannot achieve. His writings, steeped in the articulation of faith as lived experience, beckon readers towards an introspective journey, encouraging a heartfelt encounter with the divine.

Similarly, Hopkins' poetry, resplendent with the fervor of his religious conviction and his awe before nature as a manifestation of God's beauty, acts as a testament to the sacramental view of life. The vibrancy of his language and the innovation of his technique—sprung rhythm, in particular—serve as a vessel for theological contemplation, enabling a palpable sense of God's presence in the mundane.

Their works collectively argue for an engagement with faith that transcends mere intellectual assent. It is a calling to witness—to embody one's beliefs in the very essence of one's being and creative output. "Let your light so shine before men, that they may see your good works, and glorify your Father which is in heaven" (Matt. 5:16). Newman and Hopkins exemplify this through their fusion of life, literature, and theology.

Within the scope of the challenges facing the contemporary believer, the resonances of Newman's and Hopkins' thought are profoundly pertinent. In an age often characterized by fragmentation and secularism, their integration of faith and art offers a beacon of coherence—a path to navigate the complexities of modern existence.

For the Christian intellectual, and indeed for any individual seeking to intertwire faith with vocational callings, the lives of these two men provide a blueprint. Newman's emphasis on the moral obligation to utilize one's talents in service to God, and Hopkins' embodiment of this through his poetry, illuminate a path of evangelization that is deeply authentic.

Their call extends into the realm of academic and theological discourse, challenging scholars and theologians to a deeper engagement with literature as a medium of truth. It is a call to recognize the power of the written word—not only to articulate but to embody and evoke the presence of the divine.

The synthesis of their insights presents a holistic vision of literature as an act of faith. In their respective approaches, one discerns a shared conviction that literature can, and indeed must, serve as a conduit for deeper spiritual encounter and understanding. This is not literature as a mere accessory to faith, but as a vibrant, essential expression of it.

As this exploration draws to a close, it is evident that the dialogues initiated by Newman and Hopkins continue to resonate with urgency and relevance. The illative sense, as a concept and practice, remains a fertile ground for further scholarly inquiry and personal reflection. It calls for an engagement that is both intellectually rigorous and deeply infused with a sense of divine mystery and wonder.

The relevance of Newman and Hopkins extends beyond their historical context, reaching into the heart of contemporary debates about the nature of faith, reason, and the role of literature in shaping human understanding. Their lives and work stand as a testimony to the enduring power of a faith lived out in intellectual and literary endeavor.

In the silence that follows the last quill stroke, there is an invitation—an invitation to continue the conversation, to expand the boundaries of our understanding, and to explore new pathways in the intersection of faith and literature. The journey does not end here; it merely takes on new directions, guided by the insights and inspirations of those who have walked this path before us.

The legacy of Newman and Hopkins, rich in its complexity and beauty, challenges us to a deeper exploration of our own faith journeys. It invites us to view literature not merely as a reflection of human experience but as a profound engagement with the divine—an engagement that has the power to transform, to illuminate, and to inspire.

As we lay down our quill, let us do so with a sense of gratitude for the guidance of these two luminaries. Let us carry forward their vision, blending the rigor of intellect with the depth of faith, and embracing the creative potential of literature as a means to encounter God. In this, we find not an ending, but a new beginning—a continuation of the timeless dialogue between the human and the divine, mediated through the beauty and truth of literary expression.

Appendix A: Further Reading and Resources

In the journey towards a deeper understanding of the convergence of literature and faith as seen through the lives and works of John Henry Newman and Gerard Manley Hopkins, one finds the road is both vast and intricate. The exploration does not cease with the final page of this volume but extends into a broader landscape of texts and resources. Presented herein are recommended readings and resources for those who seek to delve further into this compelling synthesis of theology, literature, and the quest for truth.

Primary Texts

To grasp the essence of Newman's and Hopkins' approaches to faith and literature, one should engage directly with their writings. For Newman, *Apologia Pro Vita Sua* and *The Idea of a University* are crucial for understanding his views on faith, reason, and the role of education in religious belief. Hopkins' poetry, gathered in *The Poems of Gerard Manley Hopkins*, edited by W.H. Gardner, showcases his innovative style and theological depth. Reading through these works, one encounters the heart of their insights, "For with the heart man believeth unto righteousness; and with the mouth confession is made unto salvation" (Rom. 10:10).

Secondary Sources

Exploring the myriad interpretations and analyses of these two figures can illuminate their contributions from various angles. *John Henry Newman: A Biography* by Ian Ker offers a comprehensive look at Newman's life and thought, providing context to his theological and literary endeavors. Similarly, *Gerard Manley Hopkins: A Life* by Paul Mariani delves into the life of Hopkins, reflecting on how his faith influenced his poetry. These biographies serve as gateways to understanding the men behind the theology and literature.

Thematic Studies

For those interested in the specific themes of Newman's and Hopkins' work, *Newman and the Word* by Terrence Merrigan and *Gerard Manley Hopkins and the Victorian Visual World* by Catherine Phillips examine how both authors interacted with the intellectual and cultural currents of their time. Such texts provide a lens through which to view their works, opening up new avenues of thought and reflection akin to the seeking of wisdom, "That the man of God may be perfect, thoroughly furnished unto all good works" (2 Tim. 3:17).

Contemporary Reception and Critique

To understand the ongoing impact and relevance of Newman and Hopkins, contemporary critiques and studies offer valuable insights. Journals such as *The Newman Studies Journal* and *The Hopkins Quarterly* regularly feature articles and reviews on the latest research related to both figures. These publications not only highlight the enduring significance of Newman's and Hopkins' thought but also how they resonate with today's challenges in faith, ethics, and literature.

Online Resources

The digital landscape provides a plethora of resources for those researching Newman and Hopkins. Websites such as the Newman Reader (newmanreader.org) and the International Hopkins Association (hopkinspoetry.com) offer texts, commentaries, and scholarly articles accessible to both academics and the general reader. These online platforms foster a community of dialogue and exploration, embodying the collaborative spirit of learning.

In this pursuit of knowledge, let us remember that the quest for understanding, much like the call of faith, is a journey that never truly ends. It is an invitation to explore the depths of God's revelation through the beauty of language and the richness of human experience, guided by the wisdom of those who have journeyed before us. As we move forward, may we do so with the light of their insights illuminating the path, "Thy word is a lamp unto my feet, and a light unto my path" (Psalm 119:105).

Chapter 13: Acknowledgments

As we journey through the corridors of this inquiry, it behooves us to acknowledge those luminaries whose insights and contributions have illumined the path we have trod. In delving into the complex interplay between faith and literature as navigated by John Henry Newman and Gerard Manley Hopkins, numerous individuals and institutions have lent their support, wisdom, and critical engagement.

Foremost, we pay homage to the divine architect of all intellectual and spiritual endeavor, "In whom we live, and move, and have our being" (Acts 17:28). It is He who ordains the ends and means of our inquiries and to whom all our efforts ultimately point.

Substantial gratitude is extended to the academic milieu that has nurtured this exploration. The faculties of theology and literature across universities have provided an invaluable forum for dialogue and discovery. Their rigorous critique and passionate engagement have been indispensable in refining the arguments presented within these pages.

The archives and libraries that have safeguarded the writings and correspondences of Newman and Hopkins have been our treasure troves. The custodians of these collections have facilitated our access with an openness and efficiency that have been nothing short of exemplary.

Colleagues in the fields of theology, literature, and philosophy have graciously shared their insights, challenged assumptions, and offered encouragement. Their camaraderie and intellectual rigor have often turned the solitary act of writing into a communal labor of love and discovery.

This work has benefitted immeasurably from the rich tapestry of discussions, seminars, and conferences dedicated to the legacy of Newman and Hopkins. The organizers and participants of these gatherings have contributed to a deeper appreciation of the nuances and complexities in the interaction between faith and literature.

Our readers, particularly those within the academy—college professors, theologians, and literary scholars—deserve special mention for their engagement with this text. Their discerning questions and thoughtful reflections have prompted further exploration and refinement of the ideas presented.

The Roman Catholic Church, by preserving the heritage and wisdom of its saints and scholars, has provided an enduring context for understanding the theological underpinnings of Newman and Hopkins' work. The Church's commitment to the synthesis of faith and reason has been a guiding light in this endeavor.

Critical voices from within the secular and non-Catholic spheres have enriched this dialogue, reminding us of the universal reach and relevance of our subject matter. True understanding often flourishes in the soil of diverse perspectives and honest debate.

Research assistants and graduate students have contributed their energy, skills, and fresh perspectives, helping to navigate the vast sea of literature and to bring clarity to complex ideas. Their diligence and enthusiasm have been an invaluable asset to this project.

Family and friends have provided the necessary support and understanding, encouraging perseverance through the inevitable challenges and moments of doubt. Their faith in the value of this work has been a source of strength and motivation.

The financial support received from various grants and fellowships has been crucial in enabling dedicated time for research, writing, and travel. These resources have afforded the opportunity to engage deeply with the subject matter and to consult widely with experts in the field.

Lastly, we acknowledge the mysterious work of the Spirit, which, akin to the wind "bloweth where it listeth" (John 3:8), has guided this exploration in directions unforeseen and has breathed life into the effort of articulating the confluence of faith and literature in the lives and works of Newman and Hopkins.

In the panoramic view of acknowledgments, it becomes evident that this book is not merely the product of an individual's toil but a testament to the collaborative spirit of inquiry that binds us in our search for truth. It is our hope that this work contributes to an ongoing dialogue that enriches our understanding of the divine, nurturing a faith that seeks understanding and a literature that communicates the ineffable mysteries of God.

As we conclude this volume, let it stand as an offering—a humble contribution to the vast ocean of discourse on faith, literature, and the profound ways in which they intersect to illuminate the human condition and the divine reality that envelops it. May the thoughts presented herein inspire further reflection, dialogue, and discovery in the years to come.

Glossary

In the pursuit of clarity, it's paramount to define the bedrock upon which this discourse stands. The lexical selections herein are not merely words; they are the emissaries of meaning, woven into the fabric of our exploration of faith through the lens of John Henry Newman and Gerard Manley Hopkins. Each term is a key, unlocking the deeper understandings required by our audience of college professors, Roman Catholics, literary scholars, and theologians.

Illative Sense: This term embodies the intuitive process by which the human intellect transitions from disparate observations to coherent truth. It's a journey from the seen to the unseen, guided not just by empirical evidence but illuminated by a brilliancy that transcends mundane analysis. As written in Romans, "For the invisible things of him from the creation of the world are clearly seen, being understood by the things that are made, even his eternal power and Godhead" (Rom. 1:20).

Literary Assent: A profound, almost sacramental act of belief, where truth is not only acknowledged by the mind but embraced by the heart through the medium of literature. It's here that the spiritual intersects with the script, where divine whispers are discerned in human words, echoing the sentiment that "faith cometh by hearing, and hearing by the word of God" (Rom. 10:17).

Moral Agency: Represents the capacity to act with reference to right and wrong, emphasizing the individual's responsibility towards ethical conduct. It's a theme that finds resonance with the Pauline exhortation to "prove what is that good, and acceptable, and perfect, will of God" (Rom. 12:2), enlightening the path of one's moral journey.

Sprung Rhythm: A revolutionary metric innovation by Hopkins, embodying the natural cadence of speech while highlighting the poet's enchantment with God's creation. It's poetry that dances to the rhythm of the cosmos, urging us to see the divine brushstrokes in the mundane.

Sin and Redemption: A dual theme that traverses the landscape of Christian doctrine, reflecting humanity's fall from grace and the divine pathway back to reconciliation with God. It's a narrative of hope and renewal, where "if we confess our sins, he is faithful and just to forgive us our sins, and to cleanse us from all unrighteousness" (1 John 1:9).

Sacramentality: Deeply ingrained in Catholic theology, this concept refers to the presence of the divine in the physical, where material elements become conduits of grace. It reflects a world imbued with God's presence, affirming that "the Word was made flesh, and dwelt among us" (John 1:14), highlighting the incarnational reality of faith.

Literary Evangelism: The use of literature as a means to convey the Christian message, advocating for a truth that seeks not just the mind but the soul. It's an approach that mirrors the parabolic teachings of Christ, where stories became the vessel for divine wisdom.

Witness of Beauty: This phrase captures the notion that beauty itself testifies to the existence and nature of God. It's an aesthetic apologetic that aligns with the Psalmist's declaration, "The heavens declare the glory of God; and the firmament sheweth his handywork" (Ps. 19:1).

The Illative Imagination: A concept marrying the intuitive leaps of the illative sense with the creative embodiment found in imagination. It suggests that in the acts of creating and interpreting literature, one engages in a form of reasoning that is both imaginative and inferential.

Contemporary Literature and Theology: Refers to the ongoing dialogue between literary expression and theological insight in the modern era. It underscores the evolving nature of this discourse, acknowledging its adaptability and relevance in contemporary contexts.

These definitions serve as the foundation upon which our exploration of Newman and Hopkins is built. They anchor our discussions, providing a lexicon through which we engage with deep theological and literary themes. In embracing these terms, we step into a realm where faith and intellect coalesce, where divine mysteries are approached through the beauty of human expression.

As we delve deeper into the respective methodologies and contributions of Newman and Hopkins, these terms illuminate our path. They are the signposts that guide our analysis, ensuring that our dialogue remains grounded in a shared understanding. It's through this glossary that we embrace the complexity of our subjects, offering a clearer lens through which to view the rich tapestry of faith, literature, and morality woven by these two towering figures.

In the spirit of intellectual and spiritual inquiry, this glossary stands as a testament to the depth of exploration undertaken in this book. It invites readers into a deeper contemplation of the divine, mediated through the human experience of language, literature, and belief.

Thus, armed with this glossary, we proceed on our journey through the interwoven narratives of Newman and Hopkins, each term a stepping stone towards a fuller understanding of their approach to faith in God. It's a pilgrimage of the mind and soul, guided by the shared lexicon of our quest.